DISCOVER THE MYSTERY OF FAITH

"In a time when very few things feel stable or sustainable, my friend Glenn Packiam takes us back to the sacred, bedrock truths of our faith. Glenn is a prophetic pastoral voice that calls us to the deep with both word and song."

Brady Boyd, senior pastor of New Life Church

"In *Discover the Mystery of Faith*, Glenn invites those who have been unknowingly malnourished on the consumeristic, 'Happy Meal' faith that is so prevalent within Evangelicalism into a historically richer, Christ-centered, and more robust way of worshipping and believing."

Michael Gungor, singer/songwriter
and producer and leader of Gungor

"Glenn Packiam has written a timely book that speaks to a generation that is longing for a faith that is, in the words of St. Augustine, ever ancient, ever new. *Discover the Mystery of Faith* shows us how the Spirit is using historic worship and prayer to shape and form our faith. Read it and rediscover how ancient practices of worship can help you live out your faith in the postmodern world."

Winfield Bevins, pastor and author of *Creed:
Connect to the Essentials of Historic Christian Faith*

DISCOVER THE MYSTERY OF FAITH

DISCOVER THE MYSTERY OF FAITH

HOW WORSHIP SHAPES BELIEVING

GLENN PACKIAM

David C Cook®
transforming lives together

DISCOVER THE MYSTERY OF FAITH
Published by David C Cook
4050 Lee Vance View
Colorado Springs, CO 80918 U.S.A.

David C Cook U.K., Kingsway Communications
Eastbourne, East Sussex BN23 6NT, England

The graphic circle C logo is a registered trademark of David C Cook.

The website addresses recommended throughout this book are offered as a
resource to you. These websites are not intended in any way to be or imply an
endorsement on the part of David C Cook, nor do we vouch for their content.

Unless otherwise noted, all Scripture quotations are taken from the Holy Bible,
New International Version®, NIV®. Copyright © 1973, 1984 by Biblica, Inc.™ Used
by permission of Zondervan. All rights reserved worldwide. www.zondervan.com.

ISBN 978-0-7814-1043-4
eISBN 978-1-4347-0702-4

© 2013 Glenn Packiam

The Team: Alex Field, Amy Konyndyk, Nick Lee, Caitlyn Carlson, Karen Athen
Cover Design: Thom Hoyman
Cover Photo: Joel Stayer and iStock

Printed in the United States of America
First Edition 2013

2 3 4 5 6 7 8 9 10

081816-CS

CONTENTS

FOREWORD

One afternoon I received a call from my friend John Hartley at Integrity Music.

"I have a great worship leader, named Glenn Packiam, who is making an album of liturgical songs. Would you be interested in cowriting with him?"

John knew I would be more than "interested."

I founded and led a nondenominational church that, over a ten-year period, drifted away from an attractional style of worship to one that was more liturgical. We carefully set the prayers and creeds passed down to us by the church fathers to contemporary music. Our sung Eucharist became the summit of our weekly worship. I leaped at the chance to spend time with someone who shared a similar passion.

A few weeks later, Glenn and I met in Nashville. Our mutual hope that the contemporary church would discover the transformational power of the liturgy and Eucharist forged an instant friendship between us.

We also wrote two songs. It was a good day.

As I travel the country, it's clear that a movement is afoot. Worship leaders are exhausted. The weekly pressure to plan and deliver innovative, seismically moving, crowd-sustaining worship services is unsustainable.

Essential and far-reaching questions are surfacing: is contemporary worship compassing people toward a transfiguring encounter with God or pandering to our culture's addiction to peak experiences, entertainment, and celebrity? Has the word *relevant* become code for "keep the customer satisfied"? Do services designed around catchy themes address the longings of people in search of a spiritual narrative that will make sense of their lives? Have we become more focused on "Lights, Camera, Action," than on "Father, Son, and Holy Spirit"?

More importantly, might reclaiming the liturgical practices and theology of worship of the early church help guide our much-needed course correction?

In this marvelous primer, Glenn Packiam demonstrates how important his voice is in this emerging conversation. In a theologically rich, gracious, yet clear-eyed way, he addresses these questions and many more. It couldn't be timelier. Anyone who cares about worship and the contemporary church would be wise to read, mark, and learn from its pages.

Ian Morgan Cron,
speaker and bestselling author

CHAPTER 1

A PAUPER'S MEAL

The table was sparse, with only a green knitted circle for a place mat. On it was a porcelain dish bearing the words *Do this in remembrance of Me*. A large dinner roll sat safely within its borders. A ceramic cup held the grape juice off to the side. As I stood at this table, remembering not to rest my arms on it lest I spill more grape juice, I looked into the faces of the men and women I had come to know as my congregation.

We had just finished sitting in silence, allowing the Spirit to bring to mind the broken places in our hearts. We had then prayed a prayer of confession. On that Sunday, it may have been an adaptation of Psalm 51. Or it may have been the prayer of confession from the *Book of Common Prayer*. We had just looked at each other in the eyes and announced, as priests in Christ, that God has forgiven our sins in Jesus's name.

Now, as I stood at the table, about to recite the words that have been said of the bread and the cup countless times over the centuries, it hit me:

I've never really stopped leading worship; I've just changed where I stand.

My earliest memories of worship music are from early Saturday mornings. My dad, whose conversion to Christ had been radical and beautiful, was convinced that the best way to be a priest to his family was to blast the latest *Hosanna!* cassette from our living room before the rooster crowed. We lived in the suburbs, so there was no rooster to compete with, but were one to appear, he would have been beaten to the punch. As if the music itself wasn't loud enough, my father chose to sing along with it, adding a little Eastern vocal slide in the gaps of the melody, rendering the song atonal at best. My sister and I had no chance to sleep in.

I took piano lessons as a boy, and I dreaded them. My disciplined and responsible sister, three years older, mastered the scales and required exam pieces with gusto. I hated practicing, and the teacher frequently rapped my knuckles with a ruler for poor form on the keyboard. Most piano students in Malaysia learned piano from the Associate Board of the Royal School of Music based in London—which is a fancy way of saying that we spent half the year practicing two exam pieces and scales to perform for an examiner who flew in from England, and the other half of the year memorizing theory trivia to pass the theory exam. Royal Pain in the You-Know-What would have been a better name for it.

But I had good teachers who, despite the rulers-on-knuckles bit, worked hard to get me to practice. I did well enough to pass but found no joy in it. (Does a child find joy in anything that requires work?) I wanted to quit music.

Then, when I was ten, my family moved from Malaysia to Portland, Oregon, where my parents went to Bible school. It was there that I became transfixed by "worship music" in a church service. We joined a church with a strong emphasis on worship, led by skilled musicians who paid attention to the Spirit's work. I'm sure all that played a part in my budding love affair with worship music.

But there was also Steve. Steve was a good-looking youth leader in his twenties who was single and highly eligible. Every girl in youth group had a crush on him. You knew because every time he preached, the altar (in a nondenominational church, that's what you call the front of the church by the stage) would be flooded. By girls. Crying. All hoping Steve would pray for them.

But Steve's aura went beyond his winsome smile, tan skin, and frosted mullet tips; he could sing! Oftentimes he would get up on the keyboard and belt out a "spontaneous song" that made all the girls spontaneously weep.

As a nerdy kid who was the only foreign student in the whole middle school, I adored Steve. *If I could be like Steve, I would be cool! The girls would like me! I wouldn't just be a kid from Malaysia.*

Years later, when I found myself standing on the stage of a large arena with thousands of teenagers, leading "worship" as part of the Desperation Band, I must have subconsciously felt that I had realized that goal. I was now Steve (I never thought this, but I know I felt something like this). Until a group of pimply-faced teenage girls approached me after the session. I bent down from the edge of the stage, confident that they were going to ask for an autograph—or at least for prayer. They asked, instead, what was wrong. I was confused. *What was wrong? Nothing! I'm a rock demigod. What could be wrong?*

"What do you mean?" I said.

"Well, your face on the JumboTron looked so terrified. We thought you were afraid, so we started praying for you."

I am not Steve.

———————————

We moved back to Malaysia right after my eighth-grade year, and though I had just been finding my way with friends in Portland, my three years in America gave me near-celebrity status with my peers in Malaysia. This newfound popularity came at the right time for my confidence. When you're a teenager, confidence plus influence equals leadership. So leadership was granted to me.

I welcomed it but wasn't sure that I was cut out for *worship* leadership. Nevertheless, at the urging of one of the other teen leaders, I agreed to lead worship for a junior-high youth service a month or so away. Nearly every night leading up to the scheduled service, I lay my head on my pillow and dreamed up new song lists, fitting together different songs in different keys and tempos.

The day came. I led worship and loved it. And I never looked back. Eventually, I began leading worship for our youth group and spent many a Saturday "training" our worship teams in both the theology and practice of leading worship. My friends and I even formed a little team that went out to nearby small towns to do weekend worship workshops and mini-conferences. We were young, and there was a purity to what we were doing, an innocent love for God's presence and a desire to see others experience God in a powerful way.

I left for college right before I turned eighteen. Going back to America felt exciting, but going alone was frightful. I'll never forget my first chapel at Oral Roberts University. I was sitting in the balcony, singing along, and was overcome by the sense of God's presence. The worship team was wonderful, and I wanted in. A few auditions and several weeks later, I was part of the team. It was through our involvement in ORU Music Ministries that Jon Egan, Jared Anderson, and I—among many other talented people—got to know and trust each other. Those years are full of memories of long worship services, extended "ministry times," and meaningful conversations about what God might call us to do and be. It would be years later that Jon and Jared and I would find ourselves part of New Life Church, forming the Desperation Band.

When Gary emailed me, he sounded like he was looking for a fight. But there was something undeniably true about what he had written. He had been to church that morning and wanted me to know that he had heard the name of Jesus only twice, the Trinity referenced not at all, and a slew of worship songs addressed to a generic "You" that could just as easily have been applied to Simba, the Lion King.

I wrote back to him explaining that this was just poetry. Worship songs were merely artful expressions of a deeply held faith, a faith that was rich and robust, a faith articulated in all the doctrinally correct ways. He sent me a link to an article in *USA Today*—or some paper like it—citing a survey that indicated most American evangelicals had no idea what they really believed about Jesus, the incarnation, or the Trinity, nor were they sure that any of it mattered. Running out of rebuttals, I managed some feeble argument in response.

The next email contained, as I remember it, only a Latin phrase: *lex orandi, lex credendi*. I asked, in a slightly irritated way, what it meant. He told me to Google it. So I did. And I was plunged into a world that I had already been moving toward.

The phrase *lex orandi, lex credendi* means, quite literally, "The rule of prayer is the rule of faith." Maybe a better way to think of it is, "The way you pray and worship becomes the way you believe."

This sounds simple enough, but stop for a moment and think about it. If you're anything like me, you've spent most of your life thinking of prayer and worship as an expression of the faith that is in our hearts. There is certainly something true about that. Our prayers and our worship do, indeed, reflect the faith in our hearts. It is an overflow of it. But in another sense—*perhaps a larger sense*—prayer and worship form our faith. Worship doesn't just reflect our faith; it is what shapes our faith.

The Latin phrase is an old phrase the Church has passed on through the centuries. My ecclesiastical ancestors knew something I didn't know (and this wouldn't be the last time I came to *that* realization). Worship—*how we pray and sing corporately as the gathered people of God*—shapes believing.

But if this is true—and I started to believe that it was—then I had a problem.

I thought about the gnawing feeling I had had every time I stepped onto a stage at a large event to "lead worship." I felt a certain tacit hypocrisy in our claim that we were there to lift up Jesus, when there we stood on an elevated stage, with multicolored lights aimed at us and cameras magnifying our faces on giant screens. Really? Were we *really* there to lift up Jesus? Then why was I self-consciously thinking about how I dressed or how I moved onstage, with or without a guitar in my hands? Of course, our deepest intentions were pure. We wanted desperately for people to experience God's presence. It wasn't our fault that event organizers wanted to hype things up or script a worship experience.

I am honored to call some incredible worship leaders and song-writers my friends. I know how tormented they feel about the stages on which they sometimes find themselves. You see, a funny thing happened to worship music on its way to the radio charts. But that is a tale for another book, and for another author (like Michael Gungor in his book, *The Crowd, the Critic, and the Muse*).

What I felt was bigger than the tension between the sometimes-greasy underbelly of the industry and the many good people who work within it with pure and noble aims. I began to think there was something deeply wrong with the *way* we led people into worship. I know. This is a massive claim, and I didn't want to believe it at first. In fact, I hadn't even realized it until my Latin-phrase-emailing "friend" ripped the veil from my eyes.

You see, when I met Gary, he described himself as a "recovering atheist." He had, in fact, been one of the poster dads in our church—an ORU alumnus, a New Life small-group leader, and a veteran short-term missions-trip leader. But in 2006, his faith fell apart. Collapsed, as he puts it. He wasn't just wrestling with doubt; he became a full-blown atheist, and an obnoxious one at that.

In the years that followed, his understanding of the Christian tradition was rebuilt. By retreading some very old paths, Gary began to discover a rich Christian faith, one shaped by ancient practices of worship—old prayers and prayer books, the practice of the sacraments, and more. He began to read the church fathers and learn about the wider world of Christianity. To return to pop-Evangelicalism felt, to him, like going from fine cuisine to fast food: it could fill your belly, but it was sorely lacking in both taste and nutrients.

Good, rich, Christ-centered worship is a feast. This kind of worship is a bounty of beauty and truth, with layers of flavor, textures of taste. Each course builds on the previous one, elevating the dining experience from a functional necessity to an odyssey of ecstasy. (This may seem like hyperbole, but for anyone who has eaten a multi-course gourmet meal, thoughtfully prepared and artfully crafted, you know what I mean!)

This rich worship feast is what transformed Gary's approach to faith. The more I got to know him, the more I understood where he was coming from and why what seemed like a thoughtlessly strung-together worship set list and a service assembled like a variety show bothered him. The truth is not quite as harsh. We *weren't* thought-less. We *had* a theme in mind, and lots of planning went into each Sunday. But when you compare what we were doing with how the great liturgists and theologians of church history put together their "order of worship," it's very easy to see how it looked like we were playing around in the kitchen and calling it dinner.

The more I thought about our worship services and how the way we worship really does shape the way we believe, the more I wondered, *Dear God, what have we been feeding them?* A few years later a wise older friend answered my rhetorical question:

"Glenn, we've been giving them a pauper's meal."

I was finally beginning to see.

Perhaps part of the reason the Church is malnourished and our faith is anemic is because our worship services have become a theological Happy Meal.

Jon Egan, Jared Anderson, and I formed the Desperation Band in the summer of 2002. Our church, under David Perkins's leadership, launched a youth conference that summer, with hopes that it would become a prayer and missions movement. We were the worship team for the conference and, we hoped, for the movement. By God's grace, over the years Desperation has become a movement of sorts, calling young people to seek God sacrificially and to serve Him faithfully.

I had already made the decision to step out of the Desperation Band before I met Gary. I say that to be clear: I didn't step out of our moderately influential modern worship rock band because I didn't believe in it anymore. I did, and I do. Jon and Jared wrestled with many of the same questions I did—questions that arose from being in too many surreal settings on the road, too many hyped-up environments that could be confused with the genuine and mystical sense of God's presence. I am proud to call the Desperation Band my brothers. They—Jon with the band, and Jared in his solo career—continue to lead people in refining and renewing their understanding of corporate worship in ways that are parallel to the path I've been on. I stepped out of the Desperation Band in 2008 largely because I felt that the long-term trajectory of my life lay in pastoral ministry and not in an itinerant ministry. I am a teacher. And I was getting frustrated with trying to fit mini-sermons in between songs, trying to keep an often adolescent crowd from mistaking emotional sensationalism for the genuine manifest presence of God.

But it was more than that. It wasn't just the *people* or the *context* of the events. It was *me*. I became increasingly aware of how tainted things could become because of my own ego. I liked being on stage. I liked when people knew my songs. It was becoming harder to tell the difference between the rush of an adrenaline high—from the crowds and the music and the soaring refrains—and the wind of the Holy Spirit. I needed to get off the train. At least for a bit. When Gary and I started emailing a year later, it felt like God was giving me language for my holy discontent. Granted, it was in Latin, but it was language nonetheless!

The way we worship becomes the way we believe. I was starting to believe it.

I soon discovered that there is another phrase that completes the saying: *lex orandi, lex credendi, lex vivendi.* The way you worship and pray shapes the way you believe, which in turn shapes the way you live. So, if I was starting to believe it, something about my life had to change.

More than my faith was at stake. As I stepped into a pastoral role in the fall of 2009, leading a new Sunday-night service at New Life Church, I began to meet young people whose stories were not all that different from Gary's. Sure, they may not have experienced the full collapse of their faith, but some felt enough doubt that it had left them shaky. In the '90s, our church went through the same evangelical love affair with certitude that so many other churches did. We knew the "facts" about God and life. It could all be proved. Christians were logical, and our truth was obvious. Everyone else was just dumb or degenerate or both. Everything about our "faith" could be neatly packaged and sold. And thousands bought into it.

Until they didn't. Until they realized that a God you can explain is a God you can contain. And a God you can contain can't be worshipped. So, if we are going to undo this mess, our practice of worship may just be the place to start. There is a way to pray and worship that reflects the mystery of our faith, a way that, in truth, shapes our faith to be more aware of its own mystery. I want to enter that mystery. I want to partake of that feast. And I invite you to join me in it.

You see, I haven't stopped leading worship. I've just changed where I stand.

CHAPTER 2

LEARNING A NEW LANGUAGE

Songwriting was the first casualty. I found it hard to write without tearing every phrase apart, wondering if it said enough, or if what it did say was good enough or clear enough. Or true enough. How could I teach orthodox theology through my songs?

I knew that this was an unrealistic goal. Songs are works of art, and art must work subversively. Trying to write in a systematically theological way domesticates the wildness of art and, quite honestly, the wildness of God. After all, God did not reveal Himself to us in a book of systematic theology. He comes to us in narratives and poetry, songs and stories, fiercely dynamic, terrifyingly Alive.

It would be too easy to say that everything I had written up until this point was now counted as rubbish—to borrow Saint Paul's famous phrase—in light of my worship epiphany. But it wouldn't be true. I was and still am grateful to have written the songs I did.

I'm not ashamed of them. Songs are like memorial stones in the Old Testament—they mark a point along the journey—and the songs I wrote tell the story of my faith and the faith of my community, our church. I *am* that story; those songs are a part of me and will be for a long time. To be honest, I am amazed at the grace that was poured out at every songwriting session, planned or unplanned! And I was never sloppy in my approach, at least not consciously. I always tried to source at least one or two passages of Scripture as the primary text for each song I wrote so that it would be rooted in the Bible. Many other worship songwriters take the same approach. In fact, I don't know any writers who carelessly string together lyrics.

So this angst about the theological content of the songs wasn't altogether new for me. But suddenly I saw a new gravity in the task. Thinking about congregational worship as something that *shapes* the faith of a church—and not merely as an expression of that faith— made me look at songs more seriously and more critically. It wasn't so much a "coming awake for the first time" as much as it was a new kind of alertness, a keenness of mind like the kind that results after a vigorous outdoor run or a fresh cup of coffee.

Unfortunately, my friends and fellow songwriters can probably attest to my fussiness in this season. It was hard for me to feel good about yet another worship song addressed to a generic "You." I often asked songwriters if there was a way they could work in a Trinitarian progression of thought from verse to verse. I worked on a song that tried to set N. T. Wright's Christology of Jesus as Israel's Messiah and thus the "world's true Lord" to music (it's not bad, actually). I wanted every line to pass a seminary standard, culling together the best theological reflection on that theme throughout church history.

More often than not, the results were better lyrics and stronger songs. Thankfully, I have patient and forgiving friends who, though they may have been puzzled by my fussiness, were not offended. At least, I don't think they were.

Praying someone else's words can be awkward.

My mother always wanted my sister and me to make our own cards. It wasn't a money-saving tactic; she just wanted us to take the time to craft something that would genuinely express how we felt on special occasions. Store-bought cards are fine, but they aren't as personal. She's right. As a father of four, I know there's nothing like a handwritten note or drawing from one of our children. Big scrawled letters, unevenly written; stick-figure family portraits, crayon marks outside the lines—it's all proof that they did it themselves, and that it came from the heart.

Most of us think that prepared words are insincere words. The more polished a speech or a letter is, the more formal and the less personal it feels. In order to be truly heartfelt, you should speak from the *heart*, not from your notes, even if your words suffer from a few "ums" and "uhs." You should write your own cards. And if you do it out of the blue when it's least expected, that is best of all.

Christians have a version of this, especially in charismatic circles. It goes like this: it's fine to have a service plan or a sermon outline, but when the plan gets changed or the sermon gets ditched, that's when you *know* God is moving. The Spirit, it seems, is often spontaneous. And since the Spirit is spontaneous, then He must love it when we are spontaneous. Spontaneity equals sincerity in the Spirit's "love language."

No one I knew growing up ever said it this way, of course. It was implied in the little things. Like the way we taught a new Christian to pray. "Just start talking to God," we'd say. "Prayer is just like any conversation with a friend."

Of course, this is true, at least in one sense. We have a God who is deeply personal, who desires a real relationship with us. Prayer is how we commune with God. I suspect that the simple "everyman" description of prayer that became popular in the 1970s and '80s was a reaction to churches that had made prayer seem dry through years of tired recitation. Much has been written about the growth of denominational churches in post-World War II America. But what came with the boom of these largely traditional churches was a worship form that involved reciting prayers, creeds, and confessions in church. This, to me, is a wonderful thing. But something must have happened over time. The words began to carry less meaning. Or people needed an emotion to accompany the words to make them meaningful. Or maybe it was the anti-establishment suspicions of the '60s and '70s and the desire for authenticity from people in front of microphones. Since politicians weren't serving it up, musicians did, with raw conviction and real passion. Is there anyone more emblematic of this age than Bob Dylan, with his imperfect but honest voice and his seemingly stream-of-consciousness lyrics? Maybe all of this found its way into the Church, and movements were born.

The gift of the "Jesus movement" and other such revivals of the '60s and '70s was that they taught us to worship and pray and preach as if God was really present, as if God was *near*. And He is. He speaks. He heals. He cares about our lives. He hears us when we pray and sing, even if our prayers and songs are simple. These movements were probably the necessary correctives in their day. Like the reforms in worship that took place in the late medieval Church—from the Protestant Reformations to the Catholic reforms that followed—these movements had as their aim a revitalized spiritual life for local congregations. Just as Latin liturgies in rural Europe in the fourteen hundreds were strange and unintelligible to the laity, so cold, prewritten prayers felt worlds away from the turbulent realities of the '60s and '70s.

Let's write our own prayers, someone said. *Better still, let's write our own songs.* After all, songs are just prayers set to music, right?

There are always unintended consequences that come with every movement, even a revival. Decades after the first pure flames of earnest passion, generations after the inspirational leader, come the bastardized versions of things, a cheap imitation of the ideal or the theology that began the revolution. Someone will miss the heart of the movement and build a theology out of a tangential theme, like a bad cover band playing a reggae version of a classic rock song.

———————————

I couldn't believe what I was hearing. Or seeing. The guest preacher at our college chapel instructed us all to stand, raise one hand in the air like we were reaching for a lever in the sky, and pull it down as we said—*no, chanted*—the words, "Money cometh to me now!"

Why he phrased it in King James English, I shall never know.

A third of the students mimicked the motions in jest, a third in earnest, and a third refused to do it at all. I was part of the last third. The only trick was, I was seated onstage with the other members of the Spiritual Life staff. Remaining in my seat that day was my Rosa Parks moment. Finally, I was asked to head to the piano to play under his closing prayer.

Prayer? This is prayer? More like an incantation with hand motions, I thought.

Still, the university paid me to do this, as I had come on staff as the worship leader after graduation—and I knew none of the faculty had invited this clown show into chapel. It was a decision out of the hands of any of the Spiritual Life staff. So, out of respect for my colleagues and boss, I went to the piano. But I refused to play. Or stand. Or do the hand motions. This … this … whatever-it-was wasn't prayer.

This is the trouble with telling people to pray what's in their hearts, to just talk to God the way you would talk to a friend. After decades of people never being taught *how* to pray, how to talk to the Creator and King of the world, we begin to pray in the language that comes most naturally. But selfishness is our mother tongue. Tell people to "pray what's in their heart," and they will pray selfishly. They will ask for stuff, and plead for more, and raise their hands to the sky to pull down an imaginary lever of prosperity, seeking satisfaction for their insatiable souls.

Isn't it interesting that when the disciples asked Jesus to teach them how to pray, He didn't ask incredulously, "*Teach* you? Why, you don't need anyone to teach you how to pray … just pray!" Nope. When His disciples asked Him how to pray, He taught them. More than that: He gave them a prayer.

Eugene Peterson writes in his marvelous book *Answering God* that just as we learn to speak by being spoken to, so we learn to pray by praying back to God the words He has spoken to us. Peterson isn't talking about some crazy "word from God" you "received" about winning the lottery; he means praying the Psalms. Drawing on the parallel between the structure of the Torah—*God's Word to Israel*—in five books, and the Psalter as Israel's response to God, also ordered in five books, Peterson invites us to see the Psalms as instructions in how to answer God.

I am reminded of a scene in C. S. Lewis's retelling of the ancient myth of Cupid and Psyche, *Till We Have Faces*. In a climactic moment of the story, the girl who has rehearsed her case against the gods for ruthlessly taking her sister is finally able to address the gods. There she confronts the harsh reality that she is not yet ready to speak. She says:

I saw well why the gods do not speak to us openly,
nor let us answer. Till that word can be dug out of
us, why should they hear the babble that we think
we mean? How can they meet us face to face till we
have faces?[1]

How can we hope to speak with God until we learn His language?

Holly and I have four children, three of whom can talk. Our youngest can make only sounds. They are responsive sounds, interactive noises, but unintelligible nonetheless. She's a baby, only six months old. We think her sounds are adorable. Throw in a few smiles and sudden hand movements, and we're smitten. This is our beloved child with whom we are well pleased. But if she were still making only these noises a year or two from now, we'd have a problem.

It was Lewis, again, who wrote that God is easy to please but difficult to satisfy. He is thrilled with our little signs of love, our cooing and oohing. But if we are serious about wanting a relationship with our Father in heaven, we'll have to do better than that. We'll have to learn His language. We'll need to learn how to pray.

How do we learn to pray?

How does a child learn her parent's language? By repeating back to the parent words she does not yet know, words whose full meanings she does not yet grasp. First the concrete words: "Ball." "Water." "Blankie." Then the conceptual ones: "Hungry." "Sleepy." "Thirsty." In fact, as a toddler grows, he or she learns to put sentences together not by being instructed in the rules of grammar—goodness knows English has far too many exceptions to its rules for that to work! Children begin to put words together in sentences by hearing sentences said to them. And then they repeat those sentences. Again and again. Often to a parent's chagrin.

There will be a time for originality, a time for children to practice their own creativity. But first comes imitation, and imitation by repetition. Anyone who has ever learned a skill, a second language, or an art started this way. You learn to paint by first trying to replicate great paintings. My first piano pieces were not original compositions, try as I did to put my own spin on Bach.

So if selfishness is, because of our sin-bent nature, our mother tongue, and if prayer really is a language that must be learned, and if learning happens best by imitation and repetition, then *what* are we to pray? The Psalms are language school; they train you in the language of prayer. It was Israel's hymnal, but more than that: the Psalms were the grammar school in the language of prayer for every Hebrew child.

Christians carried on the practice of psalm praying. Christopher Hall, in his wonderful book *Worshiping with the Church Fathers*, writes that the church fathers continued the practice of psalm praying because they "believed that our dispositions—our deeply habituated thoughts, words and actions—are shaped by those we listen to and imitate."[2] Far from being the "vain repetition" Jesus warned against, psalm praying for the early Christians was about spiritual formation. And the Spirit is at the center of the action. Hall writes:

> The Holy Spirit desires for us to hear these words, to meditate on them, to speak them with our tongues and hide them in our hearts. Without doubt the Spirit could have provided a different prayer book for us or no prayer book at all. Instead, the Spirit has given us the psalms.

The Holy Spirit knows we need help learning how to pray; the Spirit knows we are apt to stumble and perhaps lose our way if we exclusively rely on our own words and thoughts in prayer. The point is that it is our thoughts, words and actions that need remolding, reshaping. We need mentors in prayer, and the psalmist is one of the best. If we listen carefully, immersing ourselves in his words and life, our own disposition will change, in prayer and out.[3]

Early monastic communities, like Saint Benedict's, whose "Holy Rule" provided a portable and repeatable model that enabled Christianity to spread in rural Europe, would pray all one hundred and fifty psalms in a day! The fathers believed that "through repetition, the dispositions and words of the psalmist ... become those of the one who continually prays the psalms."[4] As a result, the church as a whole adopted this early monastic model.

Early on, Christians began to see the Psalms as a kind of language they needed to learn. But they saw it not merely as a language with which to commune with God, but as a language through which they could express what was deep inside their hearts. So prayer is, after all, an expression of our hearts! It's just that even in learning to express our hearts, we need to learn the language of prayer through psalm praying. It is the Word of God that is, to borrow Lewis's phrase from before, being "dug out" of us, so that what we say is not mere "babble."

Athanasius, the bishop of Alexandria at the beginning of the fourth century and one of the leading voices at the Council of

Nicaea, understood the power of finding the right words to pray. The famous defender of Trinitarian theology wrote about psalm praying in a letter to Marcellinus:

> He who recites the Psalms is uttering the rest as his own words, and each sings them as if they were written concerning him, and he accepts them and recites them not as if another were speaking, nor as if speaking about someone else. But he handles them as if he is speaking about himself.[5]

The Psalms, Athanasius believed, are like a "mirror to the person singing them, so that he might perceive himself and the emotions of his soul, and thus affected, he might recite them."[6]

What makes psalm praying even more powerful is the Holy Spirit, who is the living link between the prayers of the psalmist and our own hearts. After all, each psalm, Athanasius said, "is both spoken and composed by the Spirit so that in these same words ... the stirrings of our souls might be grasped, and all of them be said as concerning us, and the same issue from us as our own words, for a remembrance of the emotions in us, and a chastening of our life."[7]

Fine, fine, you might think. *But this was normative for the church fathers and monastics. Surely they couldn't expect ordinary, simple-minded working folks to actually pray this way?*

Not so fast. Jerome, a century or so after Athanasius, wrote that psalm praying was not the work of professional Christians or clergy. "Wherever you go, the husbandman sings the alleluia over his plough; the toiling harvester refreshes himself with the psalms; the vine dresser prunes his vine to a song of David," he said. "These are the popular songs of this country; the love songs of the shepherd's whistle; the lyrics of the farmer as his tills the soil with devotion."[8] Psalm praying, in early Christianity, was not optional extra credit; it was standard fare. It was how you learned the language of prayer.

Yes, but isn't all this—and perhaps you're embarrassed by the question in your head but you'll say it anyway—*too* Catholic? Simply: no. But don't take my word. Here is Martin Luther, the great Protestant reformer of the fifteen hundreds. In "A Simple Way To Pray," Luther wrote about psalm praying as a way to combat the lack of passion in his own prayer life—quite the opposite of our own instincts! Luther said:

> First, when I feel that I have become cool and joy-less in prayer, because of other tasks or thoughts (for the flesh and the devil always impede and obstruct prayer), I take my psalter, hurry to my room ... and as time permits, I say quietly to myself and word-for-word the Ten Commandments, the Creed, and ... some psalms.[9]

But do evangelicals do this? Not quite a century ago, the brilliant and brave German theologian and pastor Dietrich Bonhoeffer—who along with C. S. Lewis is a veritable evangelical "saint"—insisted that the Psalms keep us from the idleness of "praying what's in our hearts." In his instructions regarding Christian community, Bonhoeffer is his usual forceful self:

> If we are to pray aright, perhaps it is quite necessary that we pray contrary to our own heart. Not what we want to pray is important, but what God wants us to pray.… The richness of the Word of God ought to determine our prayer, not the poverty of our heart.[10]

And then there's Jesus.

Jesus, Saint Augustine believed, is all through the Psalms. "When we listen to the psalms … we must pay attention to seeing Christ, to discerning him…. Yes, he will show himself to those who seek him, he who appeared to people who were not seeking him. He who saved those who scorned him will not shun those who desire him."[11]

But Jesus is not only present in the Psalms. Jesus, more than likely, learned to pray by praying the Psalms. Imagine Jesus, talking to His Father in heaven—God from God, light from light, begotten not made, of one being with the Father, yet now incarnate. Imagine Jesus in human flesh, praying as a man, praying as Israel. Imagine Jesus praying the Psalms. It's no surprise that in His moment of deepest agony and pain, the words that come out of His lips are words He probably prayed hundreds of times before, words well-worn for any Jew acquainted with suffering, the words of Psalm 22:1:

> My God, my God, why have you forsaken me?

With His dying breaths, Jesus prays a borrowed prayer.

If our songs are juvenile, they may simply be a symptom of our adolescent faith. But maybe they are also part of the problem. Maybe our simplistic, peppy songs actually perpetuate our spiritual adolescence. That's a question that won't stop eating at me. That's why I can't stop thinking about the songs we sing, the words we put in the mouths of those who gather each week in Christ's name. The frightening reality is that in churches all across the world, worshippers *are* praying someone else's words. They pray and sing the words of today's worship leaders and songwriters. And they may be good words, but are they *God's* words?

I can't help but wonder what our songs sound like to God. Perhaps in our innocence and spiritual infancy, God is moved by the raw humility of our cry, like a mother to a baby. It's like the man Jesus described who beat his chest and cried out, "Have mercy on me, God, a sinner."

This is a pure and perfect prayer for the beginning of our faith. Then, as we grow a little, we find a few more words. There may be something charming about our sincere if also simplistic words. God, like the parent of a toddler, may delight in these passionate, heartfelt sounds.

But I wonder if after enough time, God—the God who is easy to please but hard to satisfy—is waiting for us to grow up. I wonder if in His love He keeps calling us to a deeper relationship with Him, a richer conversation, if only we would humble ourselves and learn His language. He waits for us, like the disciples long ago, to turn to Him and ask, "Lord, teach us how to pray."

And then He will speak His Word again to us, teaching us to pray it—speaking it and singing it—back to Him.

CHAPTER 3

TETHERED TO
THE NARRATIVE

There's a scene in an episode of *Little House on the Prairie* in which Pa and a friend need to walk out to the barn in the middle of a snowstorm.

"Better put the rope up," one of them says.

Now, I'm a city kid. I didn't grow up around barns and ropes. Or snow. So it took me a while to figure out what was going on here. In the harsh blizzards and whiteout conditions of the old prairie days, farmers used to put a rope up between the house and the barn so that when they finished up their chores for the day, they'd be able to use the rope as a guide back to the house. Without it, many a man would wander about in the cold and blinding snow, thinking he was walking in a straight line, only to discover that he was lost.

Even after I understood the rope-between-house-and-barn practice, it wasn't until I read Ian Cron's marvelous memoir (of sorts), *Jesus, My Father, the CIA, and Me* that I began to consider the metaphor at work here for the spiritual life. In Cron's description of a similar practice, a farmer tied a rope around his waist, tethering himself to the house while he finished up the chores. Cron describes the Eucharist as a rope tied around his waist, keeping him from wandering too far from faith.

This image also tells the story of the church in its contemporary worship journey. We have, rightly, wandered into a new world and explored new ways of communicating the gospel and expressing our worship. But the clear skies of yesteryear are filled with clouds of ambiguity. The sunshine of a world once radiant with Christian presuppositions has long faded.

Today, as the winds swirl around us, we hear many different voices from a plurality of faiths. "God" is no longer limited to the "God of Abraham, Isaac, and Jacob, the God and Father of our Lord Jesus Christ." "God" can mean a life force, the universe, an energy, a philosophical concept, or even you and me. The world in which we now wander is chillingly indifferent to our claims about Christ and the hope He represents for the cosmos. And it's getting harder to see in the midst of the storm.

We desperately need to find our way home, or at least to know which direction to go. If only there were a rope tied around our waists, something tethered to the House to guide us in the storm.

When the Council of Nicaea wrote the Nicene Creed in AD 325, it wasn't designed to be the sum total of all Christian doctrine. They formulated the creed, in part, to settle theological disagreements around key Christological and Trinitarian issues. But as N. T. Wright forcefully argued in *How God Became King*, the creed contains phrases that stand for larger themes. We should, Wright suggested, "festoon" ideas and images from the whole body of Scripture to these summary sentences in the creed.[1] When we see it this way, we understand why it is the *only* faith confession that is accepted and used by *every* stream of the body of Christ—Catholic, Protestant, and Eastern Orthodox.

I sometimes wonder why many churches feel the need to come up with their own statement of faith. Such a document, I fear, only serves to differentiate within the body of Christ in an unhealthy "us" versus "them" way. Before attempting to write a new "creed," ask yourself why. Then if you do change something, ask yourself again *why*. The damage to the unity of the body of Christ cannot be overstated. It is the Nicene Creed itself that teaches us to say, "We believe in *one holy catholic* [read: worldwide] *and apostolic Church*."

Yet the Nicene Creed cannot be reduced to an answer key or a theological checklist. It is so much more than that. In fact, the very language of the creed prevents us from treating it like a cold and dusty statement of faith.

Each section opens with the words "We *believe in* …" If we were writing the creed, we might begin each section with the phrase "We *know that* …" What's the difference between "We believe in" and "We know that"? One is about faith, the other is about fact; one is about mystery, the other is about certainty; one places you inside

God, the other stands aloof and almost equal to or above God. You can say, "We know that" about the information in a dictionary or a phone book. But to say, "We believe *in*" is to place yourself within something, to put all your eggs in one basket, to set your whole life upon something or someone.

What makes the creed even more remarkable is that it does not make a proposition the object of our faith. In other words, it does not have us say, "We believe in the *doctrine* of the Trinity"; instead it says, "We believe *in God the Father* ..."

Again, *what's the difference?*

The object of our faith is a *Person*, not a *proposition*. We do not place our lives in an idea or a doctrine or a system or a set of values. We place ourselves *in* the personal God: Father, Son, and Holy Spirit. Proclaiming the creed, then, is an act of worship, not a recitation of doctrine. Faith, after all, is not simple agreement or the acknowledgment of certain propositions or hypotheses. Faith is the placing of your whole life within God, the only One who is faithful enough to hold your life, redeem it, and save it.

There is no worship without faith, and there is no faith without worship. It is faith that leads us to worship and worship that enlarges our faith. Why should our greatest, most central and unifying profession of faith, the Nicene Creed, *not* be part of our congregational worship?

The answer may have something to do with the fact that many people in the Church today have negative associations with the creed. Many people grew up reciting the creed without an ounce of faith or worship in their hearts. I cannot speak as to why this was the case. But certainly this is no reason for the Church to abandon it as part of our corporate worship.

Just because someone has badly burned a rib eye doesn't mean we should give up eating steak (goodness, no). We shouldn't remove the creed from the menu just because it was ill-prepared and sloppily served. We need the nutrients it provides. We just need a better imagination for how to serve it to our congregation.

Perhaps it's necessary to also note that others object to the creed because "it's not Scripture." This is a statement of stunning ignorance. Sorry. That's a bit blunt, I know, but it's true. You see, the council that determined the Canon—which books were Scripture and which weren't—is the same council that confirmed the creed. And many of the creedal statements had been passed down from the second century and even appear in the letters of the New Testament, which means creed and canon are intimately connected.

The creed is the rope that leads us home. It reminds us of our Story, of where we came from, of what our fathers and mothers of the faith believed.

Early Christians spoke these words of worship and belief in the face of ridicule and scorn, confessed and clung to these words even when they knew that they could lead to their deaths. The creed, after all, didn't form out of thin air at the Council of Nicaea. The words and phrases show up early in the Church's life, early enough for Paul to say that he himself is only passing on what has been given to him.

The question we must ask is this: "What sort of faith will we hand down to our children?"

If the rope is no longer tethered to the house, how will we find our way home as we wander about in the snow? And how will we lead our children there? What will keep their faith? Unless we remain tied to our Story, our faith is sure to flounder. Worse yet, it may die with us.

When I arrived at New Life Church as a "worship apprentice" (read: intern with a college degree) in the summer of 2000, worship pastor Ross Parsley suggested I join the other ministry interns on their annual hike up Pikes Peak. I thought he was joking. I've never been much of an outdoors guy, and while I enjoyed pickup games of basketball, I would never embark on an arduous mountain hike for sheer pleasure.

Nevertheless, I had just arrived in Colorado and had visions of redefining myself, of becoming a different, more adventurous version of myself. I was set on becoming a *Coloradoan*.

Around that time some new friends convinced me to get up early on a Saturday morning and stand in line at an REI garage sale. I bought a North Face backpacking tent that could withstand all four seasons and an accompanying sleeping bag filled with down to keep me warm. (I used the tent twice and the sleeping bag a few more times, but neither in any truly rugged or outdoor conditions. Driving to a neatly marked, pre-reserved campsite in the glory of the Colorado summer hardly counts!) Good idea or not, you can see I was in the state of mind to take on the challenge of hiking Pikes Peak, a thirteen-mile climb up six thousand feet to a summit of roughly fourteen thousand feet above sea level.

When we began hiking the trail in the predawn darkness, the broad and smooth path surprised me. *This shouldn't be too bad*, I thought to myself. The grade hardly felt steep. This was going to be a good walk, I felt sure.

Strangely, about two hours in, my legs got heavier. The slight grade felt like a sheer vertical climb. My backpack (a small North Face pack with clips and nets for any accessories I wanted to attach) with only a Nalgene water bottle, saltine crackers, and a PB&J sandwich felt like Christian's knapsack of rocks in *Pilgrim's Progress*. David, one of the ministry interns who had been around a few years, offered to take my backpack for me.

"No," I said. "I'm fine."

I wasn't. But I didn't want to confirm their suspicions that we worship folks were softies. An hour or so later, I looked around for David. He found me and took my pack without much resistance from me this time.

We broke for lunch about halfway up.

Okay, I thought. *So far, so good. I can do this.*

But I couldn't. The short stop for lunch fooled my legs into rest mode. From then on, every thirty minutes or so, they locked up in cramps.

Bryan, one of the leaders of the ministry interns, offered to stay with me as I hiked. We walked together, stopping every half hour to drink a bit of water and eat a few saltines to help my leg cramps. Then we came to the timberline, the point above which the air gets so thin that even trees can't breathe and therefore cease to grow.

Great. Who do I think I am? Am I better than an evergreen?

Still, with Bryan walking with me, and David carrying my backpack, I kept going.

"Look," someone said. "We're almost to the sixteen golden steps."

Ah, I thought. *This is the last stage before the summit. Sixteen steps. I can do that. My townhome has more steps than that.*

But "steps" is a cruel and misleading name for long, winding mountain switchbacks. I couldn't bear it. No way. I can't make it.

"Yes, you can," Bryan said. "I'll help you."

Seeing a large group of interns already ahead of me—*far ahead of me*—and hearing the voices of those who had already reached the summit brought strength to my weary, out-of-shape legs. As I got to the last switchback, I heard them cheering me on. I decided to run the last twenty yards. It was, as it turned out, a woefully bad decision. My hamstrings locked up one final time, sending me stumbling to the ground. Thankfully, I didn't injure anything other than my pride in the tumble.

I made it to the top at last, some seven and a half hours after we began.

That was over twelve years ago, but I keep coming back to it. As with all epic tales of an odyssey, parallels to life and faith abound, though my hike is hardly Homeric. In *Secondhand Jesus,* I used this experience in contrast to one in which a person just stares at a map and never gets on the trail. It is certainly a kind of foolishness to know all about Christ and the Christian faith but to never actually *follow Jesus,* never take the long, arduous walk—what we sometimes call discipleship—with Him.

Yet there is another kind of folly. It is this: to embark boldly upon the journey, giving no care to the trail or to a company of hikers. Try going alone up Pikes Peak without paying attention to the trail, and you'll get lost. In fact, in the Boy Scouts of America's list of hiking safety rules, these two stand out:

- Never hike alone … use the buddy system.
- Stay on the trail.

So it is with faith. We cannot walk alone. We need others to travel with us. Fortunately, we have them. As the Lord reminded Elijah, there are *always* others. We are never the only ones. And if we think we are, we should take heed: *something is amiss.*

Moreover, there *is* a trail. We need not pretend that we are the first people to walk this journey with Christ. Thankfully, others have walked before us, following the risen Jesus into the world He is redeeming.

Proclamations like the Nicene Creed remind us that we are not the *first* and we are not the *only.* It is also important to remember that the creed is not the only proclamation that does this for us. There is also the Lord's Prayer and many of the aforementioned creedal formulas or statements in Paul's New Testament letters. There are the old Hebrew prayers and the Psalms, as we explored in the last chapter. There are also the early Christian songs—based on Mary's song (the *Magnificat*), Zechariah's song (the *Benedictus*), and Simeon's song (the *Nunc Dimittis*).

All of these are old, well-worn words, prayed by mothers and fathers and sons and daughters in times of trial and on occasions of joy. These words form a path, a trail to walk on. When we say them, sing them, or pray them with worship and faith in our hearts, we can remember how many others have prayed these words before us. We can think of the great church fathers, the bishops and theologians, the peasants and farmers, the missionaries and martyrs. We can imagine all the saints around the world who gather each week on the Lord's Day and say these very same words and sing them and pray them with one voice.

All of a sudden, we are no longer alone. We are caught up in the great company of saints, praying alongside David and Jeremiah and Paul. We realize that we are not the first to face despair or hunger or fear. We are not the only ones desperate for mercy and redemption. Our joy of being found by God's grace is multiplied in the praise of all the saints, in heaven and on earth.

We are not walking up this mountain alone.

The beauty of this truth came to me not in a Gothic cathedral or a remote monastery, but in a dusty cement building in the middle of an African village. I was on a trip to Swaziland—the country with the highest rate of HIV infection in the world—when we visited a community of orphaned and vulnerable children that our church supports through a partnership with Children's HopeChest. We greeted the local pastor who visited these children several times a week. We met the women who cooked them meals with the money that came in from our sponsorship.

And then came the children. Singing. Dancing. Playing. Thrilled with stickers and face paint and games and songs and stories and lessons, they made the afternoon pass like a heavenly moment. When one of the local ministers stood to conclude our time, she told the children that it was time to pray together.

I closed my eyes, waiting for a short, sincere prayer. Instead, in stumbling unison, their voices rose.

Our Father, who art in heaven,
Hallowed be Thy name.
Thy kingdom come, Thy will be done, on earth as it is in heaven.

My eyes opened, blurring with tears. I caught the eyes of the others on our team. We gently shook our heads, all of us thinking the same thing: *we pray this prayer ... almost every Sunday!*

Give us this day our daily bread.

Oh ... what this simple, biblical phrase meant for these children! I could never say these words the same way again.

Forgive us our trespasses
as we forgive those who trespass against us.

Like the parents who abandoned them? Like the family members who chose a life that led to disease and ultimately to their demise, leaving these children to fend for themselves?

For Thine is the kingdom,
the power and the glory, forever and ever,
Amen.

Amen. There is a rope that ties us to our Story; it is the same rope that binds us to each other. It reminds us that even in the most fearsome storm, when we cannot see and faith is all we have to guide us, we will not falter.

Others have come this Way before.

Others walk it even now.

The creed, the prayers, the Psalms, and the Scriptures … all of these bind us to the Story, tether us to the narrative of God's redemption.

May we all find our way home.

CHAPTER 4

RETELLING
THE STORY

We stood for most of the two-hour service. The only time they instructed us to sit was during the priest's homily. Even then, there were no chairs, just a woven rug on which to sit. And when we stood, we did not watch or listen. We participated, waiting for our turn to sing the replies. Fortunately the choir, which flanked the room on either side, standing perpendicular to the congregation, was well versed in the responses. Their voices were beautiful, echoing in the small dome-roofed room. The dome. I kept looking up at it. Every inch was painted, and the pictures told a story. Paintings of the saints lined the walls, moving in chronological order from left to right. In the center, up in front, was the altar, and behind it an inner chamber of sorts, modeled undoubtedly after the Holy of Holies. The service also included responsive music and specific actions and symbolic gestures. The priest wore robes meant to recall images of the high priestly robes. His going into the inner chamber to bless the sacrament and coming out to present it to us reenacted Christ's coming from heaven to earth for us. Even his beard and long hair represented a living portrait of Christ.

It was our first time to an Eastern Orthodox church.

Holly and I talked about our impressions on the way home. "They didn't cater to us," she observed. And she liked that. It's not that the people didn't care about guests. Quite the contrary. This was the most welcoming community of people we'd been in as guests. They greeted us warmly at the door and were genuinely sad that we couldn't stay for their weekly after-service potluck lunch in the adjoining room. But no part of the service put the worshipper at the center.

The liturgy—the whole structure of the service and the very words that were said and sung (except the sermon)—was a translation of the liturgy written by Saint John Chrysostom in the fourth century. And they sang it, said it, and prayed it *every week*, with few exceptions. Joining this liturgy that Sunday reminded us that "church" did not begin when we arrived; the worshipping people of God is an ongoing drama. We joined a program that was already in progress. Sitting on the floor was a way of communicating: *we are all on level ground. Your comfort can take a backseat for a few hours. There is only One who is seated on a throne.*

And the list goes on. Because *everything spoke*. And it told a Story. And the Story was of Christ and His salvation.

I realized that for all my scrutiny of worship songs and corporate prayers, I had been thinking too small. Yes, we need to be more thoughtful in our songwriting. And, yes, we could stand to learn the language of prayer from the Psalms and other prayers in Scripture. And, of course, we need creeds and proclamations that are part of our worship because of the way they keep us connected to our story as the people of God. But I started throwing these elements together in a service in a hodgepodge sort of way. It was a patchwork quilt of good elements—which is better than a ragtag band of bad elements!—but it didn't have much cohesion. And it was coming apart at the seams.

Attending the Orthodox church made me look more closely at the historic liturgies of the Church. I thought about the Anglican services I had visited. I began to read more about why those great theologians who wrote many of these liturgies did what they did. As I studied the European Reformations—because there were several, and they differed from each other—I discovered that many of the reforms applied to the worship service. Imagine that: to effect a theological change, many reformers began with corporate worship. I read most about Thomas Cranmer, the brave and brilliant mind behind the English Reformation and the architect of the Book of Common Prayer.

Here's what I learned: the people who, to say it in our parlance, "planned the service" were not creative directors or production managers; they were theologians. They weren't primarily concerned with organizing volunteers or coordinating logistics. Those things are important, but they shouldn't be the central concern. No, the people who labored over "service order" were preoccupied with the gospel—how it would be proclaimed and entered into and celebrated. My point here is not to denigrate creative directors but to show the difference between how people used to plan a worship service and how we plan them today. It wasn't an event to produce; it was a salvation story to tell. Over and over, throughout the Church's history, the brightest theological minds turned their attention to the content and context of corporate worship. Why? Because *the way we worship becomes the way we believe.*

Liturgy is not just a fancy word for "traditional worship." It carries meaning. Quite simply, it means "the work of the people." It was often used to describe a civic project, like a bridge or a public park. It is what a community builds together.

What is the work of the people of God when we gather each week in worship? It is to tell a Story and to participate in it. But, as we discovered in the previous chapter, we aren't starting with a blank slate. We inherited our faith from others. Moreover, those who came before us handed down our faith *through* certain worship practices. You might say that part of how our faith was preserved and passed on through the centuries is through *liturgy.* This should be no surprise by now, because—say it with me—*the way we worship becomes the way we believe.*

If that is true, then we ought not begin with the question "How would *I* like to design our worship service?" or even the more "customer-oriented" questions like "What kind of service would people respond to the best?" Those are valid questions, and they have their place. Many people, assuming that I prioritize questions of contextualization above questions of theology, ask if our new life DOWNTOWN "neo-liturgical" service was designed to "reach a particular demographic." Honestly, I squirm when I hear questions like that, though I understand where the person is coming from. In our American church context, it's a fair question to ask. After all, we've been trained to think first of pragmatic questions. We want to ask *how* before we ask *what*.

I suggest that the *first* question is, "How has the Spirit of God led the people of God to worship God in corporate gatherings throughout the centuries?" In short: "What were the historic liturgies like?" Before we change anything—and we *should* change things in the name of contextualization (more on that in the final chapter)—we must try to see what was good and beautiful and true about the way the Church worshipped throughout the centuries. Then when we change something, we ought to ask, "What have we left out? What have we added? What's better? What's worse?"

Or, better yet, ask, "What does our service say? Is it telling a story? What story is it telling? Whose story is it telling?"

After all, as our Eastern Orthodox brothers and sisters taught me, *everything speaks.*

———————

A good story requires tension. There must be a conflict or a crisis, something to draw us in, to make us feel and hope and long. The trouble with laying out our worship services in a narrative format is that we've forgotten where the tension lies.

What is the central tension of the gospel narrative?

It is that we, though we long to do what is right and become God-like in our love for others, consistently fall short. We quickly aspire to virtue, for this is what it means to have the *imago Dei*. Yet we discover our limitations right away, and this is what it means to be fallen. We are good but fallen, or fallen but good. Either way, we cannot be who we hope to be.

That is, without Christ. The gospel story doesn't leave us in our hopeless state. God comes to us in Christ, doing for us what we could not do for ourselves, being for us what we cannot be in ourselves. This is what we call grace. It is the most beautiful word in the world.

Yet our services, though they may praise grace and teach on grace, don't often lead us to *experience* grace. Why? Because the story we tell lacks tension. We don't bring people to the cliff. Our sermons leave people saying, "Wow. That's a great insight (or a powerful principle). I'm going to try that this week."

Try that this week?

When the apostles preached, people were cut to the heart, crying out, "What must we do to be saved?" And we want to preach in a way that allows people to readily run out and apply it?

Don't get me wrong: sermons must be fit to the world of the congregation. The Word must become flesh. We are not to give people heady lectures—something I'm all too often guilty of—and "trust God to help them apply it." We must speak *God's* Word in *our* world, as the saying goes. And there is a place for practical sermons, just as there are books in the Scriptures that are collections of wise sayings and generally true principles (Proverbs, for one). But if we leave people with the impression that they can do what God asked us to do without first pointing them to Christ and calling them to receive afresh His grace and His Spirit to change them and empower them, then our corporate worship services will fail.

When we started the New Life Sunday-night service in the fall of 2009, the goal from the beginning was for it to be a slightly different expression of worship but connected to New Life as a whole. My pastor encouraged me to shape the service around the growing convictions in my own heart—worship and liturgy and faith. He and I would continue to study together and preach from the same texts with the same overarching theme, but in our own ways. Because of his encouragement to give corporate expression to my personal journey of rediscovery, we began with many liturgical elements. We opened the service with about thirty minutes of "modern worship," led by my humble and thoughtful friend and fellow pastor Matthew Fallentine. He worked carefully to choose songs that fit the new approach. Out of our time of worship, I would come up and lead everyone through a corporate reading of the Nicene Creed. We had a time of silent confession, a corporate prayer of confession, Communion, the offering, announcements, and finally, the sermon. Early on, we had good pieces of the service, but we put them together like a variety show.

Then Jesse, one of our leaders, said, "Hey, have you ever thought about putting Communion at the end of the service, like as the response to the sermon?" During Lent of 2012, we decided to try it: six Sundays on which the sermon led into a moment of personal confession and then into Communion.

All of a sudden, there was a story to the service; it had a beginning and a tension and an end. Personal confession, you see, was the missing piece. Without confession, a sermon is just good advice. To end the sermon by giving people space to silently admit where they've tried to follow Christ *and failed* means we led them to the "crisis" in the salvation story. We brought them face-to-face with their own frailty and brokenness. Confession, though, is not about feeling bad about yourself or beating yourself up. In fact, confession is not the end, just as a good story doesn't end with the crisis point. You might say that it is at the crisis point that the story truly begins. In the same way, confession is a gateway to receiving God's grace.

Some Christians, however, want to do away with confession. They want everyone to know that God has already forgiven us for everything, so there is no need to ask for forgiveness. In one sense, this is true: God freely offered us forgiveness in Christ. We do not confess because *God* is *withholding* forgiveness; we confess because *we* have been *holding* onto our own self-determination and self-reliance. Like a person with tightly closed fists, unable to receive a gift, we too easily cling to our own efforts instead of welcoming God's grace into our lives. Confession is a way to let go. It brings us to the place where we finally admit that our hands are empty. It is in this place that Christ becomes our portion. We do not confess our sin because we hope to find a gracious God; we confess our sin because we *know* that God is gracious.

Confession is the tension in the story that we've been missing. What is the rescue scene without the crisis point that necessitates rescue in the first place? Can you appreciate the relief if you didn't know the anxiety? Can you celebrate grace without having been brought to your knees? However, confession cannot be thrown into the service like an ingredient in a Crock-Pot. It is meant to be more like a palate-cleansing *amuse-bouche* before the entrée. We can program the service elements like a late-night variety show; or we can arrange them in a story, a gospel narrative that people can enter into and reenact and participate in week after week after week. Historically, the Church has opted for the latter.

What would it look like if our services told a story, *the* Story of salvation?

After experiencing the power and richness of shaping our service in a "Gospel Story," we decided to stay with it. From the community developing at New Life Sunday Night, we launched new life DOWNTOWN, a brand-new campus in the heart of our city. It was a risky endeavor, but my pastor has a brave and gracious way of leading and empowering his team. The story of how it began must be saved for another day. But the thought was simply this: what if we took the culture and community of Sunday nights and "planted" it in a new field (that's what campus means!)? Could it open up the door for others who for whatever reason couldn't or wouldn't come up to the north end of town?

When we thought through our "service narrative" for new life DOWNTOWN, we wanted to draw from the Church's heritage while looking with fresh eyes at what it means to gather to worship. Like at our Sunday-night gatherings, which had been going for two and a half years, we wanted to be "rooted in history with room for mystery." We began on Easter Sunday 2012. Our experiment with service flow during Lent at New Life Sunday Night had been the perfect prologue. The Story we tell and reenact and enter into and participate in each week goes something like this:

- *Worship in Song*

  Our service begins with a call to worship. Here we center on Christ, set aside the busyness and distraction of the world, and come with humble and adoring hearts. The cross stands at the center of the stage, with the worship team around it, visually inviting us to come and worship the risen Christ.

- *Corporate Prayer and Proclamation*

  Here, we often pray for a need in our city or church, as it rises or as the Spirit leads us. We also regularly use this moment to proclaim together the Nicene Creed. Depending on the season of the church year, we will also pray a written prayer together. These prayers are often chosen from the Anglican Book of Common Prayer.

- *JoyTime*

  This is a time to give to God with glad and joyful hearts. We believe that giving to God should always be a joyful and sacrificial part of our worship. Because our Father in heaven is a gracious and generous God, part of being His children is learning to be like Him.

- *Scripture Readings*

  Before the sermon begins, there is a public reading of the Scriptures by different members of our congregation. Passages are selected from the Old Testament, New Testament, and one of the Gospels that correspond with the message and current series.

- *The Sermon*

- *Silent Confession*

  These few minutes of silent confession allow us to take a moment to become aware of the places in our lives and relationships where we have tried to live independently of God. We confess our sins, acknowledge our need for God, pay attention to the Holy Spirit's work in us, and surrender every part of our life and heart to Him.

- *Corporate Confession*

  We then move from personal reflection in silence to corporate confession, praying—or sometimes singing—a prayer of confession together, using an adaptation of Psalm 51 or a prayer from the Book of Common Prayer.

- *Absolution*

  After confession, we turn to one another and, as priests in Christ, announce, "God forgives your sins in Jesus's name." While we know that God forgives us, there is a power in seeing our brother or sister in Christ—who is also our friend and perhaps even a husband or wife or mother or father or daughter or son—look us in the eye and say that God forgives us. It is also powerful to be the one saying these words. It reminds us that we cannot hold on to the failures of others if God Himself does not.

- *Communion and Prayer*
From the earliest days of Christian worship, the Eucharist—the celebration of Communion—was the central symbol and the culminating moment of the Christian gathering. I'll say more about this in the next chapter. But for now, picture this: we come to the table with empty hands; Christ gives us His body and blood as our bread and cup. We invite families and friends to receive the Communion elements from the Communion tables and then return to their seats and take the elements together, praying for God's grace to abound in one another. We also have a prayer team available to minister to those in need of special grace.

- *Benediction and Closing*
We often pray the Lord's Prayer as a closing "family prayer." We believe this prayer, with its praise, petitions, and proclamations, can shape the posture of our hearts and teach us to pray "in Jesus's name." Then we sing the doxology a

cappella. Finally, I pray a short blessing prayer, often the old Jewish one, asking God to make His face shine upon us as we go forth into the world. It is not simply a prayer of blessing but a prayer of commission. Here the narrative is complete: from being called to worship, we have heard the Scripture, have confessed our sins, have received God's grace in Christ through the Spirit, and are now being commissioned back into the world.

There is plenty here to critique. This isn't final or infallible. It's just our feeble first attempt to think through our service like a narrative, to try to make *everything speak*, and to let it speak of Christ and His salvation.

My friend Gary, who was catalytic in my own journey of discovery, now comes regularly to our service downtown. He was asked to write an article about his experience there. Fortunately, he avoided the "consumer review" approach and chose to narrate the journey of worship we take each Sunday. This is how he tells the Story:

It's a quarter till ten on a recent December Sunday morning, and my family and I are headed to church in downtown Colorado Springs. After trying a few different churches in recent years, we now attend new life DOWNTOWN. The church's meeting location is in Palmer High School, the old public school near Acacia Park, adjacent to the iron statue of city founder General William Jackson Palmer mounted on his steed.

Unique in its mixing of traditions (both ancient and modern), new life DOWNTOWN lets me engage in the mystery of Christian faith. This is a bit of the story of how.

We enter through the school's main doors. There's a bike rack just outside, and it seems that some folks have biked to church this morning. Once inside, we pass a table stacked with information on dinner groups, local social causes, a book group, and other programs available elsewhere within New Life Church. My family meets with one dinner group from time to time, and I've done the book club a couple times too.

We enter the school's auditorium. The architecture clearly hails from the Works Projects Administration style of the Roosevelt administration's era, but what most catches my attention in this space is the wooden cross at center stage. With spotlights shining on it, the cross is draped in purple today, a fitting color for the season of Advent, those weeks of longing, repentance, and waiting for the arrival of Christmas's new hope.

In front of the cross is a table. It, too, is adorned in purple, and breadbaskets and the cup have been arranged for Communion. In the center of the table is an Advent wreath—evergreen boughs in a circle with white candles glowing. I am reminded that even in the dark of winter, the light of Christ shines forth. Two days ago there was yet another tragic school shooting in our nation. It's hard to make sense of it all sometimes. Today though, in our school-housed church, I pray that God's light and life might break into our cold, broken, and at times wintry-dead world.

Musicians are gathered on both sides of the cross and table. This morning the instruments are a unique mix of the mainstays of vocals, keyboard, guitars, and drums along with the textures of steel guitar, clarinet, and a hammer dulcimer. The talented musicians draw us into sacred worship with songs that are thoughtfully aligned with Advent's themes. I sing "O Come, O Come, Emmanuel" with thoughts of my job, relationships, finances, and more. I need the miracle of Jesus's arrival to appear in my life in very real ways this Christmas season.

This Sunday, on the right side of the stage is something I've never seen before at church: during the song service, two young ladies are painting on a canvas standing on an easel. A multicolored background is emerging from their work, and it seems a white dove is too. I wonder what it means or is going to mean. We're told they will finish the painting on Christmas Eve. In Advent's time of waiting, perhaps the Holy Spirit is reminding me of patience and hope.

Pastor Glenn Packiam steps onstage to lead us in prayer. On the screen is a prayer from the Anglican Book of Common Prayer. In a blending of great tradition with heartfelt petition, we mix this old prayer's fixed words with free-flowing dynamic prayer for those who have suffered such cursed loss in the recent school shooting.

Soon, different lay readers read from the Old Testament, Epistles, and Gospels. During the gospel reading, we all stand in respectful recognition that we're now hearing about the life and person of our Lord and Savior who once lived among us. During the gospel reading, I wonder how I can possibly be like Him. Often I don't do so well.

Today's sermon text is Acts 27, the same text being used at the north campus. In the sermon, Glenn draws from a mix of ancient and more recent sources—*The Hobbit*, *The Odyssey*, A. W. Tozer, and a popular scholarly online lecture. And as always, he helps us understand how the original audience of the Scripture may have heard the text. This morning, he stresses the difference between having faith "for" something and having faith "in" God—and encourages us to embrace the second kind of faith. I'm reminded that sometimes I fail to trust His goodness. This morning though, I am surrendered to the timeless goodness of a deeply loving God.

And then I'm given the opportunity to receive that goodness. In the same words that are being recited this morning by Christians around the world, I am given opportunity to speak words of confession and to acclaim:

Christ has died,
Christ is risen,
Christ will come again.

When it becomes my row's turn to receive Communion, my family goes up to a Communion table at the front of the auditorium. I receive the elements in memory of Christ's body broken for me, His blood shed for me. As others continue to process through and engage the sacred, the musicians continue: "Your love never fails, never gives up, never runs out on me." The promise is big, and I want it. And I receive it in a blend of humility and boldness.

We sing the doxology as a congregation—no instruments this time, just voices—and then, in the final prayer, we reflect upon how to take what we have received into this world so rich in need. Now it's time to go back out into that world.

Lord, come. Emmanuel. As far as the curse is found, make Your blessings flow. Your love never gives up, and may mine neither. Be in me this day, this week, this season, this life.

CHAPTER 5

ENTERING THE MYSTERY

There's something about a meal. It is the simplest and most common human practice. It is born, of course, of necessity. If we are to live, we must eat.

And yet a meal is so much more than sustenance. A carefully prepared meal requires that the cook choose each ingredient deliberately. A meal prepared for others, prepared with others, and enjoyed with others is a spiritual experience. The ordinary stuff of food and drink becomes a symbol of the joy we feel, a mile marker of moments in our lives. When there's an occasion to celebrate—a birthday, an anniversary, a wedding, a raise, a successful endeavor of any kind—a meal is often the way we do it.

When the people of Israel wanted to remember and celebrate God's greatest act of deliverance in their nation's history, they didn't preach long sermons or expound on the theological ramifications of that day. They shared a *meal*. To be sure, words and songs and prayers and sermons surrounded that meal, but the meal was the center. The meal, to use the language of the previous chapter, *spoke* the loudest. The Passover meal, with its bitter herbs and unleavened dough and roasted lamb, drew their minds to the smells and tastes of that hurried and anxious night in Egypt. And for generations after, for those who had never known the pain of an Egyptian whip or the exhaustion of a day spent making bricks in the heat, this meal was a way to reenact their Story. The meal was a remembering and a reenacting of God's great salvation.

When Jesus wanted to capture once more for His disciples what His death was about to accomplish, He didn't sermonize; He served them dinner. But it wasn't just any dinner. It was the Passover meal. Jesus wanted to share it with His disciples so He could redefine it for them. Like so many other pieces of Israel's life and story and practice, Passover got reworked. But not arbitrarily. Jesus showed that even the first Passover was a sign pointing straight to Him. *He* was the One who would lead them—*and all of humanity*—out of the truest slavery our race has known, the slavery to sin and death. And how would He do this? By letting the curse of death fall on Him. This time, it would not be the firstborn of all in Egypt who would die. Not the son of Pharaoh but the only Son of God would carry the entire weight of God's judgment. *Jesus* became like the Passover lamb, whose blood would stand on the doorposts of our hearts, covering us, causing the curse to pass over us. He would take our death so that we could have His life.

N. T. Wright cheekily remarked that Jesus, in speaking of His death, did not give us an atonement theory; He gave us a meal.

"This," He said, taking the bread, "is my body, given for you." And taking the cup, in the same manner, He said, "This is my blood, which is shed for you and for many for the forgiveness of sin."

"Do this"—both these things—"in remembrance of …" *Of what? Of Passover? Of Egypt? Of YHWH's deliverance?* Yes, but more. "In remembrance of *Me.*"

There's just something about a meal.

Isaiah, the poet-prophet who inspired Israel in its darkest days of exile, spoke of a Great Feast. It would be on "the mountain of the Lord." But this feast would be for *all* the nations. It would have the richest foods and the most refined wines. And this feast would lift the cloud of gloom from the world, the veil that covers the earth. What is the veil that covers the world? What darkness taints every earthly pleasure? It is the very shadow of death, which looms sometimes large and other times small but is ever lurking in the corner. No, at *this* Great Feast, God—the great Creator King and Covenant God—will "swallow up death forever" and "wipe away tears from all faces." His own people will no longer be ashamed (Isa. 25). What a feast that will be! Isaiah's imagery resonates centuries later in John's vision in Revelation of a Great Wedding Banquet.

What symbol, what act, what image could possibly be so powerful that it could make us remember and reenact a past event, reimagine a future hope, and receive a present promise?

There's just something about a meal.

My friend Ross Parsley—now the lead pastor of ONEchapel, a church he planted in Austin, Texas—has talked for years about what he calls the "family worship table." He wrote about it as well in a wonderful and insightful and gut-wrenchingly honest book, *Messy Church*. The idea is simple: church is meant to be like a family table, where children and parents and grandparents all gather to share a meal. Children will need to be patient and bear with Grandpa's rambling and sometimes repetitive stories, and Grandpa and Grandma and Mom and Dad will need to find a way to deal with the energy and messiness of the children at the table. Some churches would rather have a "kids' table," where the noise and the mess can be contained. But a healthy family lets the generations overlap so wisdom can be passed down and energy can flow up.

It's a wonderful picture, and over a decade ago when I first came to New Life, I benefited from the model as one of the "kids" at the table. (In fact, if you read Ross's book, you'll learn a few embarrassing stories about me in my younger years!) As I think of this outline of church as a family table, I keep returning to the question that opened this book: *what are we eating?* It's well and good for Grandpa and Grandma and Mom and Dad and the kids to all eat at the table together. Indeed, to gather the generations together for a church service is no small feat, but this is just the beginning. We must then examine the meal we serve the family. At a real family table, you may have all the generations represented, but if we're munching on popcorn and junk food and throwing back jugs of Coke, it's only a matter of time before malnourishment sets in. The older folks may get diabetes or have a heart attack, and the kids' teeth may rot and their bellies swell. The family worship table concept is step one. Healthy church life doesn't end with getting everyone to the table; that's where it begins.

So what *are* we eating at this family meal?

At the risk of stretching the metaphor too far, imagine with me that each part of the worship service is a dish, served in its own container. The songs are, perhaps, the side dish. The prayers are the salad. The service narrative is the arc of a well-planned multicourse meal. But what is the main course? Some have answered—and with good reason—that it is the sermon. For when the pastor proclaims the Word of God, Christ is preached and the gospel made clear.

As one who preaches every Sunday, I tend to agree.

But I would be wrong. The main course is the Eucharist. You see, if we want better content, we have to get the right container. Think about the meal again. If all we're eating is popcorn and junk food and Coke, then paper plates and plastic cups will do. But if we want a filet mignon, we're going to need better dishes, serving utensils, and silverware. Rich content requires more sturdy containers. And the Eucharist has been the "container" for the presence of Christ in the Church from the beginning. It's the one content-carrying piece of our service that is not reliant on human effort. Worship in song requires a skilled band and a humble yet confident leader. The sermon hinges on a gifted teacher or preacher. But the bread and the cup will always be the body and the blood.

I know. You're not convinced. Isn't Communion just "one of the ways" we worship and experience God? What makes it so special? What makes it the "container" for the "content" of God's presence? Are the bread and cup *really* the body and the blood?

In order to shed a bit more light on Communion, may I take you on a little walk through church history? We'll walk more quickly at first, but then slow down as we get to the Reformation. Grab your coat. We'll start at the beginning.

When Jesus took the bread, gave thanks, broke it, and gave it to His disciples, saying, "This is my body which is given for you," and when He took the cup, gave thanks, and said, "This is my blood of the new covenant which is poured out for you," He may not have known how the struggle over those words would divide His Church.

Justin Martyr, a church leader in the second century, insisted in his *First Apology* on taking those words literally.[1] What does "is" mean except, of course, *is*? (A closer examination of Greek syntax that shows that Jesus's words could be rendered "This, my body" and "This, my blood" came later.) From this early premise, theologians of the third and fourth century, like Cyril, Chrysostom, and Ambrose, began to suggest that the bread and the cup would undergo a "miraculous change."[2]

Still, it was not until the Middle Ages that thinkers tried to explain *how* this change transpired. By the eleventh century, "theologians commonly spoke of a change in substance occurring in the bread and wine," with the term *transubstantiation* coming into use later, around 1150.[3] But it was not until the mid-1200s that the term and its accompanying tradition achieved its final form in the Latin or Western Church, thanks largely to the work of Saint Thomas Aquinas.[4]

With Aquinas leading the way, medieval theologians began the shift by saying that the Eucharist was not only an act of God infusing grace to the recipient, but also a "human response," a sacrifice offered to God.[5] Aquinas took this teaching to its logical conclusion in his *Summa Theologica* by calling the Eucharist a "sacrificial offering" in its own right, thus paving the way for the deeply embedded medieval view that "the Mass was itself a meritorious act."[6]

It was to *this* medieval view of the Eucharist that the Reformers, beginning with Martin Luther, reacted most strongly. The Eucharist was *not* the cause of God's grace; God's loving nature is the cause for His grace. Nothing, not even our participating in the Eucharist, earns or merits grace. The Reformers also insisted that the Eucharist was not human work or sacrifice offered to God. Luther viewed the Eucharist as a sign of "God's promise given to faith."[7] This notion of the Eucharist as a sign may have its roots in the Roman context for the Latin word *sacramentum*: an "oath of fidelity and obedience to one's commander sworn by a Roman soldier upon enlistment in the army."[8] Augustine had developed this idea of the sacrament as an "outward, visible sign of an inward, invisible grace" centuries prior.[9]

So it's not the *cause* of grace but a *means* of grace. But how? How is Christ *present* with us in the Eucharist? Here the Reformers were divided. Luther, the most "conservative" of the Reformers in terms of how much he wanted to preserve of the doctrines and practices of the Church, worked with the idea of transubstantiation, changing it in a small yet profound way. For Luther, Christ was not present *in place* of the bread and the wine but *with* the bread and the wine. In Luther's view, the worshippers "ingest the Lord's body and blood *under* and *with* the Communion elements, with the substance of the physical realities."[10]

If Luther was the most conservative of the Reformers, then the most radical was likely Ulrich Zwingli. For Zwingli, Christ's presence was not in the bread and wine at all. Rather, Christ is "spiritually present" with the gathered worshippers, just as Jesus promised to be present whenever "two or three gather" in His name.[11] The focus was no longer on the words of institution from Christ—"This is my body, this is my blood"—but on His injunction to do this "in remembrance." Thus, the Eucharist became for Zwingli a "memorial meal." In American Christianity, I should note, we owe quite a bit of our heritage to Zwingli, for better or for worse, whether we know it or not.

John Calvin, a later Reformer, took a middle way. He agreed with Luther—and Catholic theologians—that Christ's presence at the Eucharist is focused on the bread and the wine, but, like Zwingli, he did not think it was a physical presence. Christ is in heaven, but the "heavenly Christ meets the believer in the bread and wine" through the Holy Spirit.[12]

The English Reformers tended to take Calvin's view, lopping off the extremes on either end: the Catholic "transubstantiation" and Zwingli's "memorial meal." Cranmer, the architect of the Church of England's first Book of Common Prayer in 1549, leaned more toward Zwingli's perspective—and the Swiss reformation with him. "This cup" must be taken figuratively, as a metaphor.[13]

Cranmer's "subtlety" and "skill" can be seen in the prayers he curated for the Communion service. Editing an old prayer by adding a key phrase about Christ's sacrifice "once offered," he then expounded on it so as to leave no room for any need for another sacrifice—from Christ or from the worshipper—for another sin or sinner. And while the words in the Catholic rite proceed to make comparisons of the Communion elements to the cross, Cranmer subtly left it out, going right to a prayer to the Holy Spirit:

> Hear us (o merciful father) we beseech thee: and with thy holy spirit and word, vouchsafe to bless and sanctify these thy gifts, and creatures of bread and wine, that they may be unto us the body and blood of they most dearly beloved son Jesus Christ.[14]

Here Cranmer went beyond what Zwingli had done by emphasizing the role of the Holy Spirit. But he also, in Zwinglian fashion, made the presence of Christ something experienced by the worshipper—"that they may be unto us"—rather than something that existed objectively. Once again, this emphasis is not secondary. This shows that for Cranmer, "the place of transformation [was] not the sacrament itself but the heart of the believer."[15]

There is one more word of note in Cranmer's Book of Common Prayer. After each worshipper receives the bread and the wine, the priest leads everyone in the following prayer:

> Almighty and ever-living God, we most heartily thank thee, for that thou dost vouchsafe to feed us, who have duly received these holy mysteries,

with the spiritual food of the most precious Body and Blood of thy Son our Savior Jesus Christ; and dost assure us ... of thy favor and goodness toward us; and that we are very members incorporate in the mystical body of thy Son, which is the blessed company of all faithful people.[16]

The words *mysteries* and *mystical* are used to describe the elements in general and the body of Christ in particular. One wonders if these words are meant to be a reference to the word used in the early Christian centuries for what we now call the sacraments. Because of the dominance of Greek in the early centuries, the Greek fathers appealed to certain New Testament texts that contain the word *mysterion*—like Ephesians 3:2–3—as the basis for calling these symbolic acts "mysteries" and not "sacraments."[17] While a sacrament may be a sign, a mystery involves room for something beyond what we can know.

In this prayer we find the best of the three traditions: the Catholic and Lutheran view of the Eucharist as a sign—*sacrament*; the Zwinglian/Swiss view of the Eucharist as a *memorial meal*; and the Eastern Orthodox view of the Eucharist as a *mystery*.

The meal is a sign; the meal is a memorial; the meal is a mystery. So how do we take on the sign and wear the pledge of faith? How do we participate in the memorial, the remembering? How do we enter this mystery?

We do so by partaking of the meal, the Lord's Supper, Communion, the Eucharist, which means "thanksgiving." For that reason, many churches call it "The Great Thanksgiving." For God has come to do for us what we could not, to be for us what we cannot. We come with empty hands; He fills us with Himself. His body becomes our bread, our portion; His blood becomes our drink, our sustenance. His grace becomes more than enough.

Thanksgiving, indeed. Thanks be to God!

CHAPTER 6

LISTENING TO THE SPIRIT

So what do we do with all this? How then should we live?

First of all, I should be clear that I don't think the answer is for all churches to simply "go liturgical." In fact, that sort of thoughtless cutting and pasting of ideas and elements is the very same sloppy thinking that got us in the mess we're in now. This isn't about tailoring an approach to your "demographic" or "target audience." Please. Let's stop that kind of thinking. And it *is* our thinking that needs to be changed.

But perhaps first we need to change our language.

The great ethicist Stanley Hauerwas famously argues that we make decisions based on the "world" that we "see" and that the world we *see* is shaped by the words that we *say*. So language matters. Call a worship service a "program," and you'll start thinking like an event coordinator and make decisions like one. Call worship a style, and you'll think of church as a marketing piece, custom fit to the customer you want to reach. This is *not* a discussion about worship "style." No, this is a conversation about what we do when we gather as the people of God. This begins by taking seriously the central claim of this book—a claim the church has held for centuries—that *the way we worship becomes the way we believe.*

So where *should* we start? Let me suggest a few exercises.

1. FAMILIARIZE YOURSELF WITH ANCIENT WORSHIP PRACTICES AND SERVICES.

This is going to sound harsh, but it's true: many of the most influential voices in "modern worship" know very little about the worship practices that the church has lived out for centuries. This ignorance of what the *Church* has said and sung in worship through the centuries disturbs me. When the Reformers made changes to the worship service, they did so with deliberate theological reflection and careful attention to what the service *said.*

Begin by reading anything from the late evangelical theologian Robert Webber, particularly his "Ancient-Future" series. He is a great "translator" of the rich content in the ancient liturgies. Pick up the Anglican Book of Common Prayer and read through the order of service for the Eucharist. Also, you might consider reading Joan Chittister's books on Benedictine spirituality. Read Christopher Hall's book, which I referenced earlier, called *Worshiping with the Church Fathers.* It's accessible and rich in content. And maybe better than all these books, go and visit a few churches that practice a historic approach to worship. Go to an Eastern Orthodox church and sing with them through the Divine Liturgy that Saint John Chrysostom wrote over fifteen hundred years ago. Go to a Catholic Mass. Attend an Anglican service. Or go find a Lutheran church. Check out a traditional Good Friday service, where the room is dark and the altar is covered. Ask to meet with the priests—from each of these churches—and ask them to explain why they do what they do and where it all began. I'm sure they'd be happy to talk to you.

2. REFLECT ON WHAT WE'VE CHANGED AND WHY.

Before evaluating each practice, just train your mind to notice the differences. Journal it. Mark down as many things—from the visual layout to the spoken words to the songs—that are different from your own worship tradition (and yes, "modern worship" too now has a form, a predictable pattern).

As you ask why you've made changes, be suspicious of the pragmatic reasons. Don't be easily satisfied with answers such as, "Because it works!" or "It's reaching people!" Remember that as followers of Jesus we don't gauge our success by results but by faithfulness to Jesus Christ and His remarkably different kingdom. His is a new way to be King, a new way to think about power and strength. Our grid is not numbers, so our goal is not "influence." As a pastor now, and as a worship leader from time to time, I measure my life and ministry by how faithful I have been to the Jesus Way. Don't sacrifice the theology and content, the beauty and the narrative of our services on the altar of pragmatism. Think beyond what works.

3. THINK ABOUT YOUR CONTEXT.

Context matters. Knowing your city and your people is important. I know I'm emphasizing theological reflection, but for the Word to become flesh, for us to live as the people of God *here and now*, context matters. Just as every good gardener must know the soil he works in, the field he is working, so every laborer in the kingdom must know his or her people. Developing a "theology of place" is a needed corrective to our notions of a free-floating spiritualized Christianity. The gospel does not work in a sterilized laboratory; it works within the dirt of our world. Jesus came not as an angelic being or a generic "human," but as a Jew, a descendant of Abraham and of David. God works from within.

So think about the particularities of your people. I've had people tell me that they could never use written prayers or the creed or even call Communion "the Eucharist" because of the baggage or the negative associations people in their area have with cold, unbelieving rituals or burdensome, angry religion. I get it. Others have told me that they had never prayed a written prayer corporately before, but doing it before Communion made them weep. I get that, too.

Who are your people? What "language" do they speak? How can you translate the rich, Christ-centered content and practices that the Church has said and sung and lived for centuries into their common, marketplace words? How can you retell the story of creation and fall and redemption and restoration in the services you hold?

And while we're talking about context, let me say this: there is *no* perfect context.

There is no perfect place in which to do ministry, either as a worship leader or as a pastor. At some point, you'll have to accept the imperfections of the place in which you live and minister. You'll have to come to peace with the negative associations or assumptions that others—less thoughtful others, perhaps—will attach to you *because* of your context. Trust me. I'm a pastor at a "megachurch" with worship leaders—myself included—who are on a record label in the "Christian music business." Whenever people throw stones, a few are bound to come our way. But here's what I believe: you can be faithful to Christ and His way wherever you are. And you can be an agent of change from within. I could list several influential voices within "modern worship" who diligently work at their craft and take seriously the role of placing words in the mouth of the Church. The same can be said for pastors who find themselves within Evangelicalism and yet are trying to effect change from the inside, gently tilting its axis for the better. After all, if everyone left to start something new and no one stayed and worked from within—*as God is so fond of doing*—the culture of churches would never change or be reformed.

But you can't do this on your own, which leads to the final thought ...

4. INVITE THE SPIRIT TO LEAD YOU.

The Spirit who filled the disciples of Jesus to carry out the mission of Jesus—the One who led the Church through the valley of death and persecution, through the dark forests of syncretism and superstition, through the wilderness of atheism and humanism—is the same Spirit with you and with me.

He breathes on our churches. Invite Him into this. Ask Him to help you shape a gathering that unmistakably reveals Jesus. After all, the liturgy is not the point; Jesus is the point. The practices are not the center; Jesus is the center. The question is, what practices, what "liturgy," or work of the people that we do when we gather in worship, point to Jesus as the center?

In the renewal days of decades past, people spoke of the Spirit like a flowing river. Let the river flow, we prayed and sang. I confess: I love that image. The Spirit flows like a river, cutting through all sorts of terrain, bringing hope and life wherever He goes. This is the image John the Revelator saw of the renewed creation. The presence of God going out like a river, healing the nations.

A good river needs banks—though if it is strong enough, it forms its own grooves, which become banks over time. I think the Spirit *has* formed banks. One of them, we can say with little hesitation, is the Scripture, the Spirit-inspired, God-breathed Word. I think the other is the sacraments—the Eucharist, specifically. It is a bank for the Spirit in the way it carries in it not only the story of Christ but the story of the Church. I suspect that if the Spirit leads you as you shape the gatherings that shape the faith of the people of God, then the Word of God will be clearly heard and the sacraments prominently seen.

So here we are. Worship is not merely the expression of our faith; it is an essential part of what forms our faith. *The way we worship becomes the way we believe.* And because we now believe that, we—pastors, worship leaders, songwriters, and worshippers—can begin to think about *how* we worship. And the question we must wrestle with by the Spirit in every context is this: how can our worship help us enter and experience together the mystery of faith?

Now, at last, we can ask, "What *is* the mystery of faith?"

The central proclamation of Christian worship throughout the centuries is, arguably, the Memorial Acclamation:

Now we proclaim the mystery of faith:
Christ has died;
Christ is risen;
Christ will come again.

This is the mystery of faith. It is Christ.

Wherever you are, whatever you do, and however you worship, may you find a way to make everything—every word and song and service and story—speak of Christ and of this mystery.

May you resist the urge to restrict it and define it.

May you and I—*all of us together*—enter it and invite others to it.

May our worship steep us in the mystery of faith.

And may this great and terrible and beautiful mystery lead us once more to worship.

NOTES

CHAPTER 2: LEARNING A NEW LANGUAGE

1. C. S. Lewis, *Till We Have Faces* (Orlando, FL: Harcourt, 1980), 294.

2. Christopher Hall, *Worshiping with the Church Fathers* (Downers Grove, IL: InterVarsity Press, 2009), 89.

3. Hall, *Worshiping with the Church Fathers*, 91.

4. Hall, *Worshiping with the Church Fathers*, 89–90.

5. Saint Athanasius, *The Life of Antony and the Letter to Marcellinus* (Mahwah, NJ: Paulist Press, 1980), 110.

6. Saint Athanasius, *The Life of Antony and the Letter to Marcellinus*, 24.

7. Saint Athanasius, *The Life of Antony and the Letter to Marcellinus*, 111.

8. Saint Jerome, *The Homilies of Saint Jerome, Volume 1* (Washington, DC: The Catholic University of America Press, Inc., 1964), xi–xii.

9. Martin Luther, "A Simple Way to Pray," www.se.lcms.org/uploads/simple_way_pray_luther.pdf (accessed February 4, 2013).

10. Dietrich Bonhoeffer, *Psalms: The Prayer Book of the Bible* (Minneapolis, MN: Augsburg Publishing House, 1970), 14–15.

11. Saint Augustine, quoted in Hall, *Worshiping with the Church Fathers*, 91.

CHAPTER 3: TETHERED TO THE NARRATIVE

1. N. T. Wright, *How God Became King* (New York: HarperOne, 2012), 264.

CHAPTER 5: ENTERING THE MYSTERY

1. Justin Martyr, *First Apology*, trans. Thomas B. Falls (Washington, DC: The Catholic University of America Press, Inc., 1948), 105–106.
2. Stanley J. Grenz, *Theology for the Community of God* (Nashville, TN: Broadman & Holman,
1994), 532.
3. Grenz, *Theology for the Community of God*, 532.
4. Grenz, *Theology for the Community of God*, 532.
5. Grenz, *Theology for the Community of God*, 533.
6. Grenz, *Theology for the Community of God*, 533.
7. Grenz, *Theology for the Community of God*, 533.
8. Grenz, *Theology for the Community of God*, 513.
9. Grenz, *Theology for the Community of God*, 513.
10. Grenz, *Theology for the Community of God*, 534.
11. Grenz, *Theology for the Community of God*, 535.
12. Grenz, *Theology for the Community of God*, 535.
13. Brian Cummings, ed., The Book of Common Prayer: The Texts of 1549, 1559, and 1662 (Oxford: Oxford University Press, 2011), xxvii.

14. Cummings, ed., *The Book of Common Prayer: The Texts of 1549, 1559, and 1662*, xxx.

15. Cummings, ed., *The Book of Common Prayer: The Texts of 1549, 1559, and 1662*, xxx.

16. The Church of England, *The Book of Common Prayer* (Oxford: The Clarendon Press, 1815), 193.

17. Grenz, *Theology for the Community of God*, 512.

Also available from Glenn Packiam
and David C Cook ...

HOW THE KINGDOM COMES
TO UNLIKELY PEOPLE

GLENN PACKIAM

CHAPTER ONE

FEELING LUCKY?

Bud had had a run of bad luck. When he was eight years old, his mother died. His father, unable or unwilling to raise him, later sent Bud to an orphanage. When he got out, he struggled to adapt to society and earn a decent living. He spent most of his adult life puttering on different jobs, from spray painting pipelines to being a cook and truck driver for circuses and carnivals. He had never owned a home or a car. Money had been hard to come by. Things had gotten so bad that he had even served a twenty-eight-day jail sentence for writing too many bad checks.

Then one day, Bud decided to buy a lottery ticket. At the time, he was on disability and had a grand total of $2.46 in his bank account. He had nothing to lose and over sixteen million dollars to win.

It happened. William "Bud" Post III won $16.2 million dollars in the Pennsylvania lottery in 1988. Luck, it seemed, was smiling on him.[1]

———

Who do you think is lucky? Who, in your estimation, has it made?

Is it the person with lots of money and Hollywood good looks? Is it the one who spends afternoons on the golf course or at the five-star health spa? Maybe it's the one with the perfect job and ideal marriage and dutiful children who make the von Trapps look like vagabonds. *Whoever it is*, you may say, *it's not me.*

When we think of a lucky person, we think of someone like Bud Post, an average guy who grew up like we did, with challenges and adversity, who somehow happened to buy the winning lottery ticket. There's just enough about *them* that makes you believe they are just like you. They may have had modest talent, sure, and a solid work ethic, yes. But they had a few big breaks you didn't have. They got *lucky.* They were born into the right family, at the right time, in the right city. They grew up with the right connections and were given the right opportunities. And *that's* how they got where they are.

We're not far off. We were this close, you say. *But then …* The divorce. The kid who got your son to try that drug that left him addicted. The cancer that came like a thief in the night and stole your wife's health and vandalized your finances. The downturn in the economy that turned into a recession. The investment you leveraged everything to make that was just a few months too late. The bubble that burst and left you mired in debt instead of swimming in wealth. You're Bud Post pre-1988, with a losing lottery ticket and no stunning reversal of fortunes.

Successful people, people who have made something of their lives, usually try to deflect any association with luck. Gary Player, the South

African golfer who won nine Majors, famously shrugged off an accusation of being lucky on the golf course by saying, "Well, the more I practice, the luckier I get." People on the outside looking in believe in luck—because they are sure that's all that separates them from the successful and because they hope that their fortunes will one day be reversed. People on the inside prefer to credit talent and hard work.

Malcolm Gladwell is known for offering a paradigm-shattering, contrarian view of social trends and behavioral norms we take for granted. In his book *Outliers*, Gladwell tackles the subject of the extraordinarily successful. The conventional view is that, if you add talent to hard work, you'll get a fairly predictable outcome: success. And because this is true for the moderately successful, we assume it's also true for the outrageously successful—the outliers like professional athletes or world-renowned violinists or Bill Gates.

Gladwell, however, demonstrates that, while all outliers have a base of talent and a history of hard work, that's only enough to get them to a certain point. What pushes them over the edge are things we may not have thought to consider, like date of birth, country of birth, access to education or technology, a family with disposable income to afford road trips and other creative-learning environments. His book is stocked with stories that make the point. Talent and hard work may get you some success, but to be an outlier, to be extraordinarily successful, you also need a little luck.

Gladwell's theory only reinforces what we've always suspected deep down: Others have it made, but not me. A deep divide runs between the glamorous, wealthy, successful people out there and the ordinary, average, unspectacular you and me. We're always on the outside looking in. And those others, well, they may not admit it, but they're just plain *lucky*.

They bought the winning lottery ticket.

If only we could be so lucky.

But that sort of luck isn't what it seems.

Bud Post chose to get his winnings in twenty-six annual payments of roughly half a million dollars. Within two weeks of collecting his first installment, he had spent over three hundred thousand of it. Three months later, he was half a million dollars in debt—thanks to, among other things, a restaurant in Florida he had leased for his sister and brother, a used-car lot complete with a fleet of cars he had bought for another brother, and a twin-engine plane he had bought for himself even though he didn't have a pilot's license.

A year later, debt wasn't his only problem. He became estranged from his siblings, and a county court ordered him to stay away from his sixth wife after he allegedly fired a rifle at her vehicle. Bud Post was Dale Carnegie in reverse: a millionaire losing friends and alienating people while accruing a mountain of debt. When his former landlady sued him for a portion of the winnings to pay off old debts, Bud was finished. The judge ruled that she was entitled to a third of his lottery winnings, and when Bud couldn't pay it, the judge ordered that all further payments of his winnings be frozen until the dispute was resolved.

Desperate for cash, Bud sold his Pennsylvania mansion in 1996 for a miserable sixty-five thousand dollars and auctioned off the remaining payments of his winnings. With a little over two and a half million dollars remaining, Bud hoped that people would finally leave him alone. But the person who created the most trouble was the one he could never escape: himself. He squandered it on two homes, a truck, three cars, two Harleys, a couple of big-screen TVs, a boat, a camper, and a few computers. By 1998, ten years after winning $16.2 million dollars, Bud Post was once again living on disability payments.

"I was much happier when I was broke," he lamented.

William "Bud" Post III died at age sixty-six of a respiratory failure, broke and alone.

An Unexpected Word

We think of luck as simply a positive reversal of fortune or chance occurrence that worked out in our favor. Like winning the lottery. Jesus sees it as far more. He knows it takes more than changing your conditions and surroundings to make you lucky. It takes more than money or comfort or success. It takes the arrival of the kingdom of God. And that is no chance occurrence.

When Jesus raised His eyes to address the crowd that had gathered that day, He must have seen some interesting people. These were not the important big-city types. Those would come later when Paul joined the team and traveled to various cities. No, these first followers were country folks. Simple, well-meaning, kindhearted peasants. Luke, the gospel writer, doesn't mention a name we might know or even a grouping—like Pharisee or Sadducee or scribe or lawyer—we might recognize other than "the disciples." This is simply a crowd. A crowd of ordinary, unspectacular people. Sure, the twelve He had chosen were there, but they may not have looked like the most promising bunch either.

So when Jesus began to speak, it's important to remember who He was looking at. He wasn't sermonizing, delivering a prepared oratory masterpiece to a mass generic audience. It wasn't a canned speech He had taken on the circuit. Jesus, full of compassion, sat on the plain and spoke. To *them.* To the unlucky, to the outcast and insignificant, to the overlooked and undervalued.

To *them.*

And He began with this word: "Blessed."

Except it wasn't quite that word.

Both Luke and Matthew chose the Greek word *makarios* to capture our Lord's opening word in the Beatitudes.[2] *Makarios* simply means "fortunate, happy." In secular Greek literature, it is used to describe the blissful state of the gods. It is not an inherently religious word.[3] The Greek word more like our words "blessed" or "blessing" is *eulogia.* *Eulogia* is often used to invite or invoke God's blessing and also to bless God. That word was, of course, available to Jesus—and Luke and Matthew. But He—they—chose *makarios* instead.

In the Septuagint, the Greek translation of the Hebrew Old Testament—the version of the Scriptures many in Jesus' day would have used—*makarios* is the word used most often to translate the Hebrew word *asar.* But *asar* is not the word for a "God-blessed" person or thing or action. In fact it is rarely used of God blessing anything or anyone.[4] *Asar* is simply "happy, favored, prosperous" and has the connotation of one whose paths are straight, which is a way of saying someone for whom things always unfold neatly and nicely.

The psalmist in Psalm 1 uses *asar* to say, "*Blessed* is the man who does not walk in the counsel of the wicked or stand in the way of sinners or sit in the seat of mockers." It's also the word the queen of Sheba used when she exclaimed, "How happy your men must be!"

as a way of praising Solomon (1 Kings 10:8). Even though *asar* has the implication, by the context of its use, that God is the true source or reason for the person's blessedness, it is not inherently a religious word. It's a marketplace word, used to simply say that a person is fortunate, that he "has it good."

If we were to use a word today for *makarios*, we would choose the word *lucky*. Not *lucky* as in the result of randomness. Not *lucky* as in the reward for properly acknowledging a superstition or a charm. It is neither the product of erratic chance nor the result of currying favor with some capricious god. It is simply *lucky* as we use it conversationally: *You lucky dog, you get to take a vacation next week!* Or, *Lucky you! You just got a promotion in the middle of a recession!* *Makarios*, as one New Testament commentator suggested, is akin to the Aussie slang, "Good on ya, mate," which is rather like the American, "Good for you!" Which are both like saying, "Lucky you!"

The irony of this word choice is heightened when we imagine Jesus looking at these ordinary, unspectacular people and exclaiming, "Lucky you!" He might as well have said, "Lucky are the unlucky!"[5]

> *Lucky are you who are poor,*
>   *for yours is the kingdom of God.*
> *Lucky are you who hunger now,*
>   *for you will be satisfied.*
> *Lucky are you who weep now,*
>   *for you will laugh.*
> *Lucky are you when men hate you,*
>   *when they exclude you and insult you*
>   *and reject your name as evil, because of the Son of*
>   *Man.*[6]

Why would Jesus say that? Why would He call these unlikely and unlucky people, *lucky?*

An Unlikely People

The Jews of Jesus' day knew that they were the lucky ones. They were Abraham's descendants. They were the insiders. They were God's special covenant people.

Abraham's family had been chosen to be God's people—by grace! And because it was Abraham's descendants who were enslaved in Egypt, God heard the cries of *His* people and sent Moses to rescue them—again, by grace! Then, after they had been chosen as God's people, after they had been saved from Egypt, Moses gave them the law.

The law was not how they became the covenant people of God; the law was how they were to live as the covenant people of God. For the Jews of the first century, the Mosaic law itself was not seen as a means of *becoming* God's people; rather it was a sort of badge of honor displaying that they *were indeed* God's people. You might say that the law was a sign of their luckiness. And yet the law was also a clear reminder of how far they had fallen short. They were well aware of their transgressions against the law. Even worse, their history was stained by their covenant unfaithfulness. Still God's steady faithfulness to Israel remained. And because of that, hope that Israel would be "lucky" again—that they would be delivered from their enemies, be freed from exile, and have their calling fulfilled—was alive in their hearts.

All that history and drama of privilege and failure and faithfulness and hope and expectation are the backdrop for Jesus' most famous sermon, the Sermon on the Mount found in Matthew 5—7 and the condensed but parallel Sermon on the Plain in Luke 6. The Sermon consists of quite possibly the most written-about passages of Scripture in church history.

One of the most common views is to see the Sermon as a new law. There are indeed striking parallels between the story of Moses and the story of Jesus. Moses came out of Egypt, went through the waters of the Red Sea and the wilderness on Sinai, and ascended the mountain and came down with the law; Jesus came out of Egypt (as a child), went through the waters of baptism and the wilderness of temptation, and ascended the hill[7] to deliver this sermon. Matthew's phrase "He opened His mouth and began to teach them" (5:2 NASB) is not filler. It's a Hebrew idiom to denote one who speaks with divine authority, one who utters the very oracles of God. The view of the Sermon as a new kind of law can help us see something that was likely part of Jesus' point: He means to say, to those who thought they were so good at keeping Moses' law, that unless they kept it even in their hearts they would not enter the kingdom. This is certainly clear in Matthew 5:20 when He says, "Unless your righteousness surpasses that of the Pharisees and the teachers of the law, you will certainly not enter the kingdom of heaven." In the later sections of the Sermon on the Mount, when Jesus says, "You have heard … but I say unto you …," it becomes clear that Jesus meant for them to internalize the law of Moses. The truth is, the law was always meant to be internalized, written on their hearts, and obeyed out of love for God and neighbor. Moses had said as much in his day, and later the prophets revisited the theme. Jesus, revealing the Father's intent, was giving the final word. It's not enough not to murder; you cannot hate. It's not enough not to commit adultery; you cannot lust. And so on. For the first listeners, the Sermon would have led them to realize the futility of their efforts and to respond with some version of the question "Who can live like this?" And that would have been exactly the thing Jesus was after—to show that no one could truly fulfill the law alone.

This is where some of our modern teachers have made the mistake of throwing the whole thing out. "It's all there just to frustrate us, to lead us to a Savior who will forgive and redeem us," they say. But that is only half true. Jesus does mean for us to live in the way He describes in His Sermon: He wants us to be righteous from the inside out. In fact, if we draw a parallel between when and why the Mosaic law was given and this so-called "new law" of Christ, the point becomes clearer. Just as the Mosaic law was given to a people who had already been chosen by grace and saved by grace, so for those who are in Christ, this new, inside-out way of living is for those who have already become God's people by grace. It would be impossible to treat it as simply good moral advice and discouraging to attempt to obey it as a means of "getting in." Jesus meant for His Sermon to be viewed as the way to *live* as the people of God, not the way to *become* the people of God. The great teachers throughout church history, from Chrysostom and Augustine in the fourth and fifth centuries to Luther and the Reformers in the sixteenth century, understood that the entire Sermon must be read from the perspective of one who has already been saved by grace through faith. Martin Luther said, "Christ is saying nothing in this sermon about how we become Christians, but only about the works and fruit that no one can do unless he already is a Christian and in a state of grace."[8]

Because we are in Christ, we are now the covenant people of God regardless of our ethnicity and national identity. We are "in"—by grace! We are rescued—by grace! Feeling lucky? *But wait.* There's more. We have received the Holy Spirit, which means that living this way—this way of inward righteousness—is not merely up to our own strength. We don't simply say, "Thanks, God. I'll take it from here." It is God's design that, once we are saved through Him, we receive the power, through His Spirit, to actually become the kind of person He is describing.

The Sermon, far from being a list of conditions for entry in the kingdom, is an elaborate description of how this new people of God, empowered by grace through the Holy Spirit, are to now live. Not only have we—outsiders and onlookers—been brought into the kingdom because of Jesus; now, *because* we are in the kingdom, because we are living under God's rule, this is the kind of life that God the Spirit produces in us.

Feeling lucky, yet?

Unexpected Outcomes

This is all well and good for the bulk of the Sermon on the Mount and the Sermon on the Plain, but what about the first few verses of each, the Beatitudes? Some have suggested that the Beatitudes are a "ladder of virtue," an ascending list of qualities to be attained, a sort of growth chart for the Christian. But that would make persecution the final stage in our maturation, an idea that would have made perfect sense in one era and none in another. And it would create a sort of hierarchy, distinguishing between the "serious" followers of Christ who obey the full list and the "casual Christians" who choose not to.

Others have said it is a pronouncement of the way things are, an unveiling of the mystery of life. But this would be odd, for we know that not all who mourn are comforted. And the daily news is proof that the meek never inherit much of anything.

Many teachers have taken a more moderate path, shying away from calling them a ladder of virtue or a pronouncement of the way things are and seeing them, instead, as prescriptions on how to live. Should we pursue poverty and sorrow and persecution? To read the Beatitudes as blessings that are being given because of something these people have done requires a sort of spiritualizing of the text. We would have to take being "poor in spirit" as a way of saying "morally bankrupt" and make "mourning" synonymous with "repentance." We would emphasize that to "hunger and thirst for righteousness" is to desire and long for the kind of inward "rightness of being" that only God can give us in Christ. This sort of reading of the Beatitudes has been emphasized through the centuries, from Augustine in the fourth century to the esteemed Dr. Martyn-Lloyd Jones in the twentieth century, and with good reason. It is hard to miss the progression from admitting our state of spiritual poverty to mourning in repentance to beginning to crave for an inward righteousness, and so on. Reading the Beatitudes as blessings on certain spiritual virtues would certainly be consistent with what the Scriptures teach us about growing in Christ.

But the bulk of writing and teaching on the Beatitudes has zeroed in on Matthew's list rather than Luke's. Luke's list is half the size of Matthew's (four instead of eight) and leaves no room for reading it as a list of spiritual virtues. Luke simply has Jesus announcing blessing on those who are "poor," not those who are "poor in spirit"; those who "hunger now," not those who "hunger and thirst for righteousness"; those who "weep now," and who are hated, excluded, and insulted. Luke's rendering is terse and dry. They resist spiritualization and require another way of hearing them—not a way that is in conflict with the much-written-about way, and not a way that was altogether absent in the historical expositions, just one that is not as heavily stressed. Often overshadowed by Matthew's spiritual "Blesseds," Luke's shorter, sparser Beatitudes suggest another lens for Jesus' words:

What if Jesus was announcing blessing on these people not *because* of their state but *in spite* of it?

Could it be that Jesus is not saying, "Blessed are you *because* you are poor," but rather, "Blessed are you *in spite* of being poor, for the kingdom has come to even such as you"? Reading it this way begins to make more sense. In this light, those who are mourning are now blessed because they will—in God's kingdom that Jesus is bringing—be comforted. They are not considered lucky because of their mourning; they are lucky because they are receiving—and will receive in fullness—the unexpected good fortune of God's comfort in spite of their mourning now. The focus of the blessing—especially in Luke's gospel—is on the latter portion of each Beatitude, not on the opening phrase. Luck is not in their initial conditions—of poverty and hunger and mourning and persecution—but rather in their unexpected outcomes: The kingdom of heaven in its fullness, comfort, and reward is theirs.

Dietrich Bonhoeffer, the German theologian who paid a great price for living out his convictions and opposing an immoral military regime in World War II, wrote a landmark book called *The Cost of Discipleship*. Experiencing the high cost of following Jesus and His teachings in his own life, Bonhoeffer has us read these words of blessing in the shadow of the cross. Referring to Luke 6, he wrote:

> Therefore Jesus calls His disciples blessed. He spoke
> to men who had already responded to the power

of his call, and it is that call that made them poor, afflicted and hungry. He calls them blessed, not because of their privation, or the renunciation they have made, for these are not blessed themselves. Only the call and the promise ... can justify the beatitudes.[9]

Only the call and the promise can justify the beatitudes. Not their condition but Christ's call; not their poverty but God's promise. Perhaps Bonhoeffer was echoing his German theological forefather Martin Luther, who also would not narrow his reading of the Beatitudes as merely a list of virtues. In Luther's lectures on the Sermon on the Mount, he pointed out that the people—even the crowd in Matthew's gospel and not only the disciples in Luke's—are not being praised for being poor or for mourning. Those are not virtues in and of themselves. They are being called blessed because the kingdom of God has come *even to such as these.*

The Beatitudes are chiefly an announcement, a proclamation that now, because of Jesus, everything will be different. Indeed it is already becoming different. If we can use our modern conversational expressions, we might sum up Jesus' message like this: "Lucky you, for the kingdom of God has come to the unlikely and the unlucky."

And yet.

There *is* something about being the unlikely and unlucky, the marginalized and the overlooked, that sets us up perfectly to receive what God is offering. By paying attention to what that is, we can gain the right posture of heart even if our earthly circumstances are grand and prosperous. It does, to an extent, like the rest of the Sermon (whether in Matthew or Luke), paint a picture of the type of person we become when the kingdom comes to us, the type of life God's reign will produce in us. That is how we make sense of the blessing in Matthew's Beatitudes on the pure in heart or the peacemakers.

To keep this book within my scope, I will not attempt to add to the already rich and historic writing on Matthew's Sermon on the Mount. Instead I will constrain our conversations to the four Beatitudes found in Luke's gospel. This will help our focus to be on how the unlikely have become lucky because of what Jesus has done and is doing in us. As we talk, in the chapters that follow, about each of the four Beatitudes in Luke 6, we will unpack two dimensions: how these particular people are lucky *in spite* of their conditions, and how their precise conditions *prepare* them to surrender to God's reign. Woven through our conversation will also be a recovery of the call that comes with the blessing: Since we've become the lucky ones, we must become carriers of this blessing to others who are unlikely and unlucky in our day.

For now it is enough to see that these people, the unlikely and the unlucky, are suddenly lifted to the level of admiration—*how happy for you!*—because the kingdom of God has come to them. This is Christ's announcement: The kingdom has come to unlikely, unexpected people. And for that, they are lucky indeed. Lucky with a capital L.

The Message

When Eugene Peterson, known now as the translator of the well-known and well-loved *The Message* Bible, pastored in the Baltimore area, there was a woman who came in a bit late, sat at the back, and sneaked out before the service was over. She had never been to church before. She was in her forties, and she dressed like a hippie whose time had past, but the joy on her face was new. Her husband was an alcoholic, her son a drug addict, and her friends relentless in persuading her to come to church. Week after week, she repeated this pattern of being fashionably late in arriving and serendipitously early in leaving.

Then Peterson taught a series on the life of David. One week in the midst of it, she decided to stay. The benediction was spoken, and there she was, still in her seat. When Peterson stood at the doors to greet people on their way out, she came to him with a look of astonishment. "Pastor, thank you. I've never heard that story before. I just feel so lucky," she said. Week after week, this became her new tradition: to greet the pastor on her way out and say, surprised by the hope, the forgiveness, the redemption she had learned were hers, "I feel so lucky."

It was that experience that made Peterson want to use the word *lucky* as the opening word of each Beatitude in his new translation. But he was not particularly well-known then, and the publishers were already taking an enormous risk allowing for such a modern colloquial translation. The editors got nervous and suggested he stick to the conventional word *blessed* even though the Greek *makarios*, as I've already noted and as Peterson insists, is not a "religious" word. It is a street-language word, not one reserved for hymns and prayers and blessings from God.

Either new editors came along or Peterson earned a little more latitude. When *The Message* translation of the Old Testament Wisdom Books (Job, Psalms, Proverbs, Ecclesiastes, and Song of Songs) rolled out five years later, the word *lucky* showed up eight times. Then the rest of the Old Testament was finished, and it showed up eleven more times.

No passage to me is more beautiful than this:

> *I dare to believe that the luckless will get lucky someday in you.* (Ps. 10:14 MSG)

Lucky You

If Jesus were sitting across the table from you and said to you that you are blessed, that He counts you as lucky, what would you think? *That's crazy. No, I'm not,* you would insist. *I'm ordinary, unspectacular. And besides, I'm too messed up; I've made too many mistakes. I'm the person on the fringes, the margins, the outskirts. I'm not admired or applauded, respected or rewarded. I'm just ... me. And whatever that is, it's not* lucky.

Or you would be tempted to think—as so many TV preachers do—that what this means is that everything you touch will turn to gold. You are blessed, and from here on out, everything is going to work out right. You'll never get sick, never be broke, never be troubled again. You'll live a charmed life. Things are going to get better and better until you fly away to glory. *That's* what it means to be lucky.

Both responses would be wrong.

Jesus took an inherently nonreligious word, a word from normal everyday conversations, and filled it with divine implications. It turns out the ones we ought to call lucky are the ones God is blessing with the arrival of His kingdom. In doing this, Jesus redefined who the lucky ones are. They are not the ones culture lauds as successful, not the ones we secretly aspire to be. He turned our appraisal of the good life on its head. There is a great reversal coming; indeed it has already begun. And the ones who are receiving and participating in the kingdom of God are the ones who are truly lucky, deeply blessed.

Just like the people Jesus addressed, you are called lucky not *because* of your poverty or your hunger or your mourning or the persecution you're enduring. You are lucky because *in spite* of it, you have been invited into the kingdom. It may not mean that your circumstances will immediately change. Many who heard Jesus' words didn't go off and all of a sudden "discover their purpose" and become influential world changers. Many, if not most, of them kept farming. And fishing. And raising their kids and going about their lives.

And yet everything had changed. They had seen a glimpse of God at work. Their hope was now rooted in the belief that Messiah had come. All that was wrong was beginning to be undone.

So it is for you. God has come to you in the midst of your mess and mistakes. He is announcing His arrival into your ordinary unspectacular life and inviting you to follow, to surrender, to live in a different way. God is rescuing and redeeming the world, and you—unlikely you!—have somehow gotten in on it. The trajectory of your life has been altered. You now have a part in the future that God is bringing. Like Abraham, you have been blessed to carry blessing, to live as a luck-bearer to the unlikely and the unlucky. You are receiving and participating in the kingdom of God.

And for that *you* are lucky. So lucky!

DISCUSSION QUESTIONS

1. Who do you consider to be lucky? Who is living a charmed life? Why do you think that?

2. How does this chapter reshape your picture of the person who is to be admired?

3. How is this exposition of Luke's Beatitudes different from the way you've read it in the past?

4. In what ways are you Lucky with a capital *L?*

Made in the USA
San Bernardino, CA
02 September 2017